VIEWPOINTS®
SERIES

Africa

Other Books of Related Interest:

Opposing Viewpoints Series

Afghanistan

Canada

Iran

Israel

The World Trade Organization

At Issue Series

AIDS in Developing Countries

Is There a New Cold War?

Current Controversies Series

Immigration

The World Economy

"Congress shall make no law ... abridging the freedom of speech, or of the press."

First Amendment to the US Constitution

The basic foundation of our democracy is the First Amendment guarantee of freedom of expression. The *Opposing Viewpoints* series is dedicated to the concept of this basic freedom and the idea that it is more important to practice it than to enshrine it.

Africa

David Haugen and Susan Musser, Book Editors

GREENHAVEN PRESS
A part of Gale, Cengage Learning

GALE
CENGAGE Learning®

Detroit • New York • San Francisco • New Haven, Conn • Waterville, Maine • London

Elizabeth Des Chenes, *Managing Editor*

© 2012 Greenhaven Press, a part of Gale, Cengage Learning.

Gale and Greenhaven Press are registered trademarks used herein under license.

For more information, contact:
Greenhaven Press
27500 Drake Rd.
Farmington Hills, MI 48331-3535
Or you can visit our Internet site at gale.cengage.com

For product information and technology assistance, contact us at

Gale Customer Support, 1-800-877-4253
For permission to use material from this text or product, submit all requests online at www.cengage.com/permissions

Further permissions questions can be emailed to permissionrequest@cengage.com

Articles in Greenhaven Press anthologies are often edited for length to meet page requirements. In addition, original titles of these works are changed to clearly present the main thesis and to explicitly indicate the author's opinion. Every effort is made to ensure that Greenhaven Press accurately reflects the original intent of the authors. Every effort has been made to trace the owners of copyrighted material.

Cover Image © Sergio Pitamitz/Robert Harding/World Imagery/Corbis.

LIBRARY OF CONGRESS CATALOGING-IN-PUBLICATION DATA

Africa / David Haugen and Susan Musser, book editors.
        p. cm. -- (Opposing viewpoints)
    Includes bibliographical references and index.
    ISBN 978-0-7377-5703-3 (hardcover) -- ISBN 978-0-7377-5704-0 (pbk.)
    1. Africa--Economic conditions--21st century. 2. Africa--Foreign economic relations. 3. Investments, Foreign--Africa. 4. Economic development--Africa. 5. AIDS (Disease)--Africa. 6. United States--Foreign relations--Africa. 7. Africa--Foreign relations--United States. I. Haugen, David M., 1969- II. Musser, Susan. III. Series: Opposing viewpoints series (Unnumbered)
    HC800.A55323 2012
    338.96--dc23

                                                                    2011032931

Printed in the United States of America
1 2 3 4 5 6 7 15 14 13 12 11

Contents

Chapter 3: What Is the State of the AIDS Epidemic in Africa?

Chapter 4: What US Policies Will Best Serve Africa?

Why Consider Opposing Viewpoints?

> "The only way in which a human being can make some approach to knowing the whole of a subject is by hearing what can be said about it by persons of every variety of opinion and studying all modes in which it can be looked at by every character of mind. No wise man ever acquired his wisdom in any mode but this."
>
> John Stuart Mill

In our media-intensive culture it is not difficult to find differing opinions. Thousands of newspapers and magazines and dozens of radio and television talk shows resound with differing points of view. The difficulty lies in deciding which opinion to agree with and which "experts" seem the most credible. The more inundated we become with differing opinions and claims, the more essential it is to hone critical reading and thinking skills to evaluate these ideas. Opposing Viewpoints books address this problem directly by presenting stimulating debates that can be used to enhance and teach these skills. The varied opinions contained in each book examine many different aspects of a single issue. While examining these conveniently edited opposing views, readers can develop critical thinking skills such as the ability to compare and contrast authors' credibility, facts, argumentation styles, use of persuasive techniques, and other stylistic tools. In short, the Opposing Viewpoints Series is an ideal way to attain the higher-level thinking and reading skills so essential in a culture of diverse and contradictory opinions.

In addition to providing a tool for critical thinking, *Opposing Viewpoints* books challenge readers to question their own strongly held opinions and assumptions. Most people form their opinions on the basis of upbringing, peer pressure, and personal, cultural, or professional bias. By reading carefully balanced opposing views, readers must directly confront new ideas as well as the opinions of those with whom they disagree. This is not to argue simplistically that everyone who reads opposing views will—or should—change his or her opinion. Instead, the series enhances readers' understanding of their own views by encouraging confrontation with opposing ideas. Careful examination of others' views can lead to the readers' understanding of the logical inconsistencies in their own opinions, perspective on why they hold an opinion, and the consideration of the possibility that their opinion requires further evaluation.

Evaluating Other Opinions

To ensure that this type of examination occurs, *Opposing Viewpoints* books present all types of opinions. Prominent spokespeople on different sides of each issue as well as well-known professionals from many disciplines challenge the reader. An additional goal of the series is to provide a forum for other, less known, or even unpopular viewpoints. The opinion of an ordinary person who has had to make the decision to cut off life support from a terminally ill relative, for example, may be just as valuable and provide just as much insight as a medical ethicist's professional opinion. The editors have two additional purposes in including these less known views. One, the editors encourage readers to respect others' opinions—even when not enhanced by professional credibility. It is only by reading or listening to and objectively evaluating others' ideas that one can determine whether they are worthy of consideration. Two, the inclusion of such viewpoints encourages the important critical thinking skill of objectively evaluating an author's credentials and bias. This evaluation will illuminate an author's reasons for taking a particular stance on an issue and will aid in readers' evaluation of the author's ideas.

It is our hope that these books will give readers a deeper understanding of the issues debated and an appreciation of the complexity of even seemingly simple issues when good and honest people disagree. This awareness is particularly important in a democratic society such as ours in which people enter into public debate to determine the common good. Those with whom one disagrees should not be regarded as enemies but rather as people whose views deserve careful examination and may shed light on one's own.

Thomas Jefferson once said that "difference of opinion leads to inquiry, and inquiry to truth." Jefferson, a broadly educated man, argued that "if a nation expects to be ignorant and free . . . it expects what never was and never will be." As individuals and as a nation, it is imperative that we consider the opinions of others and examine them with skill and discernment. The *Opposing Viewpoints* series is intended to help readers achieve this goal.

David L. Bender and Bruno Leone,
Founders

Introduction

> *"We appreciate support from the outside, but it should be support for what we intend to achieve ourselves. No one should pretend that they care about our nations more than we do; or assume that they know what is good for us better than we do ourselves. They should, in fact, respect us for wanting to decide our own fate."*
>
> —Paul Kagame,
> president of Rwanda

> *"There is a lot of good news about Africa—not least evidence of considerable improvements in average quality of life across the region and of a positive role played by both governments and donors in that process. Understanding that progress and its causes is an important step in ensuring it continues."*
>
> —Charles Kenney,
> development economist

At more than 11 million square miles, Africa is the world's second largest continent. The climate and geography range from the arid deserts of North Africa to the lush tropical zones and savannas of the south. The land is divided into fifty-four nations that collectively are home to roughly a billion people. The populations are as diverse as the landscape. North Africa is dominated by Arab groups whose ancestors moved westward from the Middle East in the seventh century. Indeed, their language, culture, and Islamic faith keep them strongly tied to that region. South of the Sahara Desert, which geographically separates North Africa from the rest of the continent, reside mostly black indigenous people whose Bantu-speaking forebears spread from the western part of the continent and settled the grasslands, rain forests, and dry steppes to the south and east.

It is difficult, then, to speak of Africa in any unified terms or to make broad generalizations. North African nations with their access to Mediterranean shipping lanes and trade routes that extend into the Middle East generally enjoy a higher standard of living (based on per capita income) compared with their counterparts in sub-Saharan Africa. However, even in the north, discrepancies exist. For example, a country such as Egypt has a gross domestic product (GDP, a measure of the total value of goods and services produced) twice the size of its western neighbor, Libya. Still, Libya's GDP is ten times that of Zimbabwe and twenty times that of Togo, two countries in the south. Thus, when most experts speak of problems in Africa, their concern focuses on the sub-Saharan region where the majority of nations are struggling with disease and lack of health care, spotty educational opportunities, food insecurity, and slow economic growth.

Sub-Saharan Africa remains the poorest global region. According to the Hunger Project, 41 percent of sub-Saharan Africans live on less than a dollar per day. Lack of industry, few educational facilities, poor roads, environmental degradation, government corruption, and civil wars have for decades plagued the forty-eight countries that constitute this part of the continent, keeping whole populations mired in poverty. In a 2004 paper for the United Nations Millennium Project, Jeffrey Sachs, a noted Columbia University economist, and fellow researchers argue that sub-Saharan Africa's poverty cannot be overcome from within. In the report, titled "Ending Africa's Poverty Trap," Sachs and his colleagues state, "Africa's extreme poverty leads to low national saving rates, which in turn lead to low or negative economic growth rates. Low domestic saving is not offset by large inflows of private foreign capital, for example foreign direct investment, because Africa's poor infrastructure and weak human capital discourage such inflows." To counter this cycle, the authors insist that the international community must offer more development aid to the region to ramp up what economic capacity exists in these impoverished nations.

For more than four decades, Western governments, charities, and investment organizations have been pumping billions of dollars into sub-Saharan Africa. According to the Congressional Research Service, US foreign aid to Africa quadrupled from $1.2 billion in 2006 to $6.7 billion in 2010. While Sachs has long been a proponent of foreign aid and its power to do good in developing nations, other critics have more recently argued that foreign aid is hurting African nations by funding corrupt governments and discouraging private entrepreneurship. In a March 21, 2009, *Wall Street Journal* article titled "Why Foreign Aid Is Hurting Africa," author and economist Dambisa Moyo claims, "A constant stream of 'free' money is a perfect way to keep an inefficient or simply bad government in power." In her opinion, "[African] governments need to attract more foreign direct investment by creating attractive tax structures and reducing the red tape and complex regulations for businesses. African nations should also focus on increasing trade."

Whether African countries will or even should take such advice remains a subject of debate. Some believe opening African markets to more foreign trade will compel Africans to rise to the challenge of competition and lift the economy through innovation and hard work. Critics fear that the opening of markets has removed vital protections from key economic sectors such as agriculture, forcing small African businesses to compete at a disadvantage against giant Western corporations. The result of such lopsided trade has been the ruin of native industries, these critics maintain. Paul Kagame, the president of Rwanda, has insisted that leveling the playing field for international trade would help ensure that Africa will succeed in the future. In a November 2, 2009, article for *The Guardian*, a UK newspaper, Kagame predicts, "All would benefit if the world focused on increasing investment in Africa, and if Rwanda and the rest of the continent worked to establish more equitable international partnerships. A trade relationship built on this new approach would be more helpful in reaching what should be our common goal: sustainable development, mutual prosperity and respect."

The fortunes of sub-Saharan Africa are the chief concern of *Opposing Viewpoints: Africa*. While not ignoring the diversity of this vast region, the authors of the viewpoints compiled in this book examine the problems of the region and debate what should and should not be done to improve the lot of those millions of people who, in an age of modern marvels and relative prosperity, still contend with water and food shortages, the slow spread of electrical power, civil warfare, high infant mortality rates, the dire effects of disease, and lagging economies. In four chapters—How Is Africa Faring in the Twenty-First Century? Does Africa Need Foreign Aid? What Is the State of the AIDS Epidemic in Africa? and What US Policies Will Best Serve Africa?—African and foreign commentators assess the state of the sub-Saharan region and offer advice on the policies that guide its growth in the early twenty-first century. Some insist the region still needs assistance from foreign powers to help build infrastructure that will propel it forward in a globalizing world; others believe the time has come for Africans to steer their own course, taking advantage of the talent and resources that the continent offers and the world desires. The world will be watching as Africa fights to surmount its shortcomings and embrace its strengths.

OPPOSING
VIEWPOINTS®
SERIES

CHAPTER 1

How Is Africa Faring in the Twenty-First Century?

Chapter Preface

Assessing the fortunes of Africa as a continent is a difficult task. North Africa, which is dominated by Arab cultures, has always maintained some degree of prosperity because of strong economic ties to Europe and the Middle East. The black-populated countries south of the Sahara Desert, however, largely have struggled to build viable economies while facing civil wars, disease, hunger, and other ills associated with poor resource sharing, unstable governments, and lack of education and health care. The disparities between North and South are evident in the gross domestic product (GDP)—the total goods and services produced—of various African nations. For example, the GDP of North African nations, such as Egypt and Algeria, is roughly ten to fifteen times higher than that of most sub-Saharan countries. Only South Africa, which remained closely connected to Britain, has enjoyed the economy of a developed nation—though its wealth resides mainly in the hands of its white citizens while the country's black population still subsists in poverty.

Since the 1970s, the process of globalization—the opening up of national markets to world trade—has impacted African economies. Some analysts believe free trade is helping African GDPs by increasing exports and securing more foreign interest in African markets. In a 2005 report prepared for the World Bank Conference on Development Economics in Dakar, Senegal, finance professors Lemma W. Senbet and Isaac Otchere emphasize their belief that African nations cannot afford to restrict this policy of openness. "Increasing development of capital markets and accelerated financial sector reforms are vital avenues for integrating Africa in the global financial economy and attracting international capital," Senbet and Otchere assert. They contend that African nations must continue to build financial infrastructure and attract foreign investment or fall behind a globalizing world.

Detractors contend that opening Africa's markets to global competition simply leads to stagnation of local production. Faced with a tide of cheap goods from industrialized nations, African businesses have struggled to keep afloat, these critics maintain. They claim the West is interested only in dumping goods on African markets and extracting specific resources such as gold and oil from the land. In a summer 2008 article for *Soundings*, professor of African Studies Ray Bush argued that the GDP growth rates in many sub-Saharan African countries are skewed by the global demand for oil that has fostered drilling throughout the continent. He argues that "free trade is a euphemism for northern economic dominance" because African markets seem to have to play by the rules established by industrialized nations, and these rules are, in his view, favoring the developed nations more than the developing ones.

In the following chapter, various commentators debate the economic well-being of Africa as well as improvements in standards of living that may or may not result from economic growth and foreign aid. Some of these authors bemoan the fact that rampant poverty and poor health care keep millions of Africans in destitution. Others point out that Africa is progressing slowly but surely, using modern global networks and simple entrepreneurship to build prosperity from the ground up.

> *"There is a lot of good news about Africa—not least evidence of considerable improvements in average quality of life across the region and of a positive role played by both governments and donors in that process."*

Africa's Fortunes Are Improving

Charles Kenny

In the following viewpoint, Charles Kenny quotes commonly held beliefs about Africa and then refutes them. He argues that Africa as a whole is not a backward continent trapped in despair by disease and poverty. While Kenny acknowledges that many Africans (primarily sub-Saharan Africans) still live on less than a dollar a day, he points out that more modern conveniences—such as cell phones and television sets—as well as common commodities are widespread in African markets and homes. In addition to the increase in consumer goods, Kenny asserts that improved medical technologies are more commonplace, extending the life of even the poorest Africans and reducing infant mortality rates. With basic health care available to almost all Af-

*ricans and with education and literacy rates on the rise, Kenny
believes the continent is enjoying a better standard of living than
it was just decades ago. Kenny is a development economist and
author of the book* The Success of Development: Innovation,
Ideas and the Global Standard of Living.

As you read, consider the following questions:

1. According to Kenny, by how much has the average life
   expectancy of Africans increased since 1960?

2. What reservations does the author have about the quality of education in some African nations?

3. Why does Kenny claim the United Nations Millennium
   Development Goals are a positive force in helping to
   channel the "right kind" of aid to Africa?

"Conditions in Africa Are Medieval."

Not in the slightest. It's true that some countries in the region are as poor as England under William the Conqueror,
but that doesn't mean Africa's on the verge of doomsday. How
many serfs had a cellphone? More than 63 million Nigerians
do. Millions travel on buses and trucks across the continent
each year, even if the average African road is still fairly bumpy.
The list of modern technologies now ubiquitous in the region
also includes cement, corrugated iron, steel wire, piping, plas-
tic sheeting and containers, synthetic and cheap cotton clothing, rubber-soled shoes, bicycles, butane, paraffin candles,
pens, paper, books, radios, televisions, vaccines, antibiotics,
and bed nets.

The spread of these technologies has helped expand economies, improve quality of life, and extend health. About 10 percent of infants die in their first year of life in Africa—still
shockingly high, but considerably lower than the European

average less than 100 years ago, let alone 800 years past. And about two thirds of Africans are literate—a level achieved in Spain only in the 1920s.

"Africa Is Stuck in a Malthusian Trap."

Hardly. [early nineteenth-century British political economist Thomas] Malthus's world was one of stagnant economies where population growth was cut short by declining health, famine, or war. Thanks to the spread of technologies and new ideas, African economies are expanding fast and population growth has been accompanied by better health.

The continent of Africa has seen output expand 6½ times between 1950 and 2001. Of course, the population has grown nearly fourfold, so GDP [gross domestic product] per capita has only increased 67 percent. But that's hardly stagnation. Indeed, only one country in the region (the Democratic Republic of the Congo) has seen GDP growth rates average below 0.5 percent up to this year [2009]—the run-of-the-mill growth rate when Malthus was writing in early 19th-century Britain. And though there have been all too many humanitarian disasters in the region, the great majority of Africa's population has been unaffected. The percentage of Africans south of the Sahara who died in wars each year over the last third of the 20th century was about a hundredth of a percent. The average percentage affected by famine over the last 15 years was less than three tenths of a percent. Africa has seen child mortality fall from 26.5 to 15 percent since 1960 and life expectancy increase by 10 years.

"Good Health and Education Are Too Expensive for African Countries."

Only sometimes. Some widespread health conditions in the region—notably HIV/AIDS—are still expensive to treat. But the most effective interventions for promoting health in Africa are remarkably cheap. Breast-feeding, hand-washing, sugar-salt solutions, vaccines, antibiotics, and bed nets together save millions—and could save millions more—and none need cost more than $5 a pop. Rollout of a vaccination program, for example, has slashed annual measles deaths in the region from 396,000 to 36,000 in just six years. And though Chad isn't going to see universal college enrollment anytime soon, some very poor countries have already achieved near-universal primary education based in large part on free schooling. In Nigeria, an estimated 76 percent of children expected to be completing primary school, based on their age, did so in 2005.

That even the poorest countries can afford to provide a basic level of health services and education to all of their citizens is one reason why many African countries that are as poor today as ever have still seen considerable progress in health and education. Take Niger, a landlocked country largely made up of desert. With a per capita gross national income of $170, it was desperately poor in 1962. And it is not much richer today—income per head is just $280. Yet life expectancy has increased from 40 to 57 years over that time, and literacy rates have more than tripled.

"Adding More Schools and Clinics Is the Key to Education and Healthcare."

If only. Building schools and increasing access to medical help is a vital first step—and the thousands of new primary schools and the rollout of primary-care programs are real regional success stories that have played a big role in improving quality of life But access is only the first step. For a start, the quality of provision is often atrociously low. A recent survey of primary-school math teachers from seven countries in southern Africa found them scoring lower on math tests than their students. Also, there are social forces that play a huge role in determining outcomes. Deon Filmer of the World Bank looked at school location and enrollment data across 21 countries and estimated that if every rural household was next door to a school, it would increase attendance just 3 percent. The bigger factor is attitudes: Some survey respondents in

Burkina Faso, for example, suggested that sending girls to school was the surest way for them to end up as prostitutes.

As for healthcare, survey data from across 45 developing countries suggests that if parents were a little better educated and knew more about treatments, this alone might reduce child mortality by about a third, according to analysis by [economists] Peter Boone and Zhaoguo Zhan. That suggests the importance of education and social marketing to health outcomes. In Bangladesh, for example, NGOs [nongovernmental organizations] have encouraged the construction and use of latrines in rural areas by spreading the message that defecating in fields ends, in effect, with people eating their own feces. This approach has had more widespread success than traditional programs which just subsidized latrine construction.

"TV Is the New Opiate of the Masses."

That depends on what people are watching. More than a billion people worldwide have seen *Baywatch*, and you have to wonder whether that time could have been better spent. Still, the importance of knowledge and attitudes to development outcomes suggests a big role for communications technologies. And studies from around the world suggest TV watching in poor households can have a big impact. In Brazil, women watching soap operas on the Rede Globo network have fewer kids possibly as a result. In India, the majority of households in the state of Tamil Nadu have cable access—and according to Emily Oster and Robert Jensen of the National Bureau of Economic Research, that access is associated with greater gender equality in the household, greater female schooling, and (once again) lower fertility. In Africa, TV campaigns have increased AIDS awareness in a number of countries. And it isn't just television that can change attitudes—there have been considerable successes using community education programs to increase immunization, improve hygiene, raise land-mine awareness, and promote breastfeeding.

Africa's Poverty Is Declining

Africa is reducing poverty, and doing it much faster than we thought. The growth from the period 1995–2006, far from benefiting only the elites, has been sufficiently widely spread that both total African inequality and African within-country inequality actually declined over this period. In particular, the speed at which Africa has reduced poverty since 1995 puts it on track to achieve the [UN-established] Millennium Development Goal [MDG] of halving poverty relative to 1990 by 2015 on time or, at worst, a couple of years late. If Congo-Zaire converges to [the average poverty rate in] Africa once it is stabilized, the MDG will be achieved by 2012, three years before the target date. . . .

We also find that the African poverty reduction is remarkably general: it cannot be explained by a large country, or even by a single set of countries possessing some beneficial geographical or historical characteristic. All classes of countries, including those with disadvantageous geography and history, experience reductions in poverty.

Maxim Pinkovskiy and Xavier Sala-i-Martin,
National Bureau of Economic Research
Working Paper No. 15775, February 2010.

"Development Means Economic Growth."

It's more than that. The argument that sub-Saharan Africa is in a crisis of development is usually buttressed by grim statistics on the region's economic performance. Average per capita growth rates over the past 45 years have only just surpassed half a percentage point. About half of the people in the region still live on less than a dollar a day. They need more economic growth. But this is a limited perspective on what actually contributes to quality of life. If basic education and health services are affordable even in the poorest countries, and if there's a big role for knowledge and ideas in creating demand for these services, this suggests that income growth alone is unlikely to be a panacea.

And that's what the cross-country evidence points to as well. Economic growth is a comparatively minor factor in determining improvement in health and education as well as a whole range of other elements of the quality of life. Economist Bill Easterly's study of "life during growth" around the world found that changes in per capita income were the driving force behind improvements for perhaps three of 69 measures of broad-based development—calorie and protein intake and fixed phones per person. But for the other 66 measures—covering health, education, political stability, and the quality of government, infrastructure, and the environment—income growth was not the driving force in change. There's much more to life than money, and people concerned with development need to think more broadly if they are to help sustain Africa's progress.

The United Nations' Millennium Development Goals, which set global targets for progress in areas including health, education, and the environment alongside income, are a welcome step in this direction. Some of the targets are too ambitious for a number of countries south of the Sahara to reach by the 2015 deadline, even with continued dramatic progress. But at least they help broaden the focus of the development community beyond GDP per capita.

"Aid Doesn't Work."

Sometimes. Sure, a lot of aid to Africa is wasted, and some goes to support silly ideas or countries that can't use it well. But aid has also supported some programs that have made a real difference in quality of life—things like supporting the measles vaccination program, helping to eradicate smallpox, fighting river blindness, funding educational radio programs, building sewage networks, and providing scholarships so that poor children can afford to stay in school. Even the conclusion of the vast literature regarding aid's impact on economic growth is more positive than you might think. Researchers Hristos Doucouliagos and Martin Paldam recently conducted a "metastudy" of aid effectiveness that aggregates results from 543 estimates made in 68 papers. The exercise suggested a small positive impact of aid on per capita growth rates— though the result is a statistically weak one. And with a greater understanding of what drives development in Africa and beyond, aid could play an even bigger role.

Too many people in Africa suffer under dictatorial regimes; too many parents see their children die of diseases that can be treated for cents; too many children leave school uneducated or never make it to class in the first place. Nonetheless, there is a lot of good news about Africa—not least evidence of considerable improvements in average quality of life across the region and of a positive role played by both governments and donors in that process. Understanding that progress and its causes is an important step in ensuring it continues, so that ever fewer parents suffer the loss of a child, ever more children are educated, and an ever larger proportion of Africans can live life in peace.

> *"It is time to admit that the African re-naissance is over. Across the 48 coun-tries of sub-Saharan Africa, tyranny, stagnation, and conflict are on the march again."*

Africa's Fortunes Are Declining

Bruce Gilley

In the following viewpoint, Bruce Gilley insists that many sub-Saharan African nations are in decline in the twenty-first cen-tury. Stagnant economies, wars, and high infant mortality rates are still too commonplace across the region, according to Gilley. In Gilley's view, democracy is faltering as African leaders rewrite constitutions and build their own self-serving regimes. He main-tains the corruption and arbitrary lawmaking under such gov-ernments will keep many African nations on the decline. Gilley is a professor of political science at Portland State University and the author of The Right to Rule: How States Win and Lose Legitimacy.

Bruce Gilley, "The End of the African Renaissance," *Washington Quarterly*, October 2010. Copyright © 2010 by Taylor & Francis Group Ltd. All rights reserved. Reproduced by permission.

As you read, consider the following questions:

1. According to Gilley, how many Africans relied on assistance from the United Nations World Food Programme in 2009? About how many Africans relied on that assistance in 1997?

2. What is the APRM, as Gilley defines it, and why does he believe this initiative is failing?

3. Senegal's president Abdoulaye Wade purchased a statue from builders in what country?

Twenty years ago, African leaders and intellectuals proclaimed an African renaissance. The grim days of postcolonial Africa, they said, were over. The end of the Cold War and the growing popular disgust with misrule had created an opportunity for lasting change. In its place would come democracy, development, and peace. "Africa cries out for a new birth. We must, in action, say that there is no obstacle big enough to stop us from bringing about a new African renaissance," President Nelson Mandela of South Africa told a meeting of regional leaders in 1994.

In a nutshell, the African renaissance was an attempt to have a fruitful encounter with modernity after decades of self-destructive ones. While no targets were set, the trends were supposed to be up. For perhaps a decade or so, they were. But since the early 2000s, the trends in the region have worsened. Today, it is time to admit that the African renaissance is over. Across the 48 countries of sub-Saharan Africa, tyranny, stagnation, and conflict are on the march again.

What is troubling, besides the end of the renaissance, is that Western countries have little interest and even less leverage to effect changes in Africa. But preventing Africa's slide into oblivion is at least a pressing humanitarian issue, if not a security issue. Lives matter, and saving them will require a stiffer resolve than Western leaders showed in the 1960s and

1970s, when the last African renaissance collapsed. Do Western countries, especially the United States, have the political willpower and capacity to rise to the coming challenge?

The Return of Economic Stasis

This third and latest African renaissance (after those proclaimed in the nineteenth century and then again in the immediate postcolonial period) began with economics. Senegal, which had driven itself to penury through state intervention, signed a structural adjustment loan with the International Monetary Fund (IMF) in 1979 that ushered in an era of regional economic liberalization in the 1980s and 1990s. The Lagos Plan of 1980, the last gasp of discredited African Socialism, was replaced by the IMF's Enhanced Structural Adjustment Facility as the main driver of economic growth in the region. Generally speaking, this strategy worked well in Senegal and other African states like Ghana, Tanzania, and Uganda that actually practiced it. The number of African countries where gross domestic product (GDP) per capita growth exceeded 2.5 percent a year rose from just five in the 1980s to 30 in the 2000s.

But the recent global economic slowdown has exposed an uncomfortable truth about the African economic expansion: it was driven by one-off gains in efficiency as excessive state control wound down and markets were allowed to thrive in the midst of a global commodities boom. Africa has created no global companies during its long expansion, nor has it moved up the value-added chain. Most successful regional companies are foreign-owned or run. Now that marketization gains and frothy global commodity demand have ended, the lack of entrepreneurial-led productivity gains in Africa is showing through. Regional gross domestic product (GDP) per capita, which was growing at more than four percent a year in the 1990s and 2000s, shrank in 2009, and according to the

IMF, will return to only 2.6 percent in 2010, mainly on the back of more government spending.

In a region living on the edge of survival, that is a calamity. The World Bank puts the *additional* number of infant deaths from malnutrition in the 2009 growth slowdown at between 30,000 and 50,000. Unemployment in powerhouse South Africa (whose figures are considered reliable) reached 25 percent in 2010, uncomfortably close to the 33 percent that the post-apartheid government calculated for 1994 to document the horrors of the old system (the International Labour Organization said at the time that 20 percent was a better estimate). The Millennium Development Goals (MDGs)—set by the UN in 2000 to achieve basic education, health, and income in all developing countries by 2015—are now a pipe dream for Africa, according to the World Bank. Africa is the only region in the world that has made insufficient progress or worsened across *every single* MDG indicator over the last decade. The informal economy, which reflects weak business confidence, has actually expanded during the African renaissance, and now accounts for over 70 percent of non-agricultural employment and 42 percent of Africa's GDP.

In the meantime, the rest of the developing world has been racing ahead. Africa's share of global GDP is about 2.4 percent today, unchanged from 1980 and 1990. Under-5 infant mortality fell modestly by 22 percent between 1990 and 2008, but this has been a result of the efforts of international non-governmental organizations [NGOs] pouring resources and advocacy into Africa. In other developing regions, the declines have been far steeper—for example, a 41 percent decline over the same period in India, whose population is a third bigger than all of sub-Saharan Africa. Africa's absolute levels of under-5 infant mortality remain appallingly high (144 deaths per 1,000 births versus 69 in India) due to very basic problems of health and healthcare that could be easily solved. The UN World Food Programme (WFP) had to assist 36 million

Africans (4.5 percent of the regional population) to secure their food needs in 2009—up from 21 million (3.5 percent) in 1997. The share of Africans among all WFP beneficiaries has gone *up* slightly from about one-third to two-fifths of the global total over the same period.

Democratization in Reverse

Democratization was the second key dimension of the African renaissance. It began in Benin, the country with the most coups in Africa since independence in 1960. In 1989, long-time dictator Mathieu Kérékou renounced Marxism-Leninism and announced plans for a national conference on the country's future. In 1991, he was voted out of office. That same year, the first notable revival of the term "African Renaissance" appeared in the *New York Times* in an opinion article by American law scholar Makau Mutua, a native of Kenya. Overall, the most significant democratic gains in Africa took place between 1989 and 1995. The average democracy rating for the 48 sub-Saharan African countries, as measured by Freedom House, improved by 18 percent in those six years. The subsequent decade witnessed continued democratic gains, but at a slowing pace.

Since 2005, however, Africa has witnessed four consecutive years of overall democratic decline. The year 2010 is likely to be the fifth. It is not just that democracy is backsliding, but *where* it is backsliding too. Kenya and Nigeria, the key states of East and West Africa, respectively, have suffered democratic setbacks in recent years. Mozambique, South Africa, and Uganda—three darlings of the African renaissance—have also slipped backwards. Even Botswana, the only black African country to have remained democratic since independence in 1966, is at risk since the ruling Botswana Democratic Party has never lost an election. "The likely trajectory of the country is a downward spiral," writes Kenneth Good, a professor of politics at the University of Botswana for 15 years, in the new book, *Democratization in Africa: Progress and Retreat*, whose subtitle reflects the gloomy expert consensus on the trend.

Even the all-too-familiar coup is back in fashion—in Togo in 2005, Mauritania and Guinea in 2008, Madagascar in 2009, and in Niger in 2010—after a period in the 1990s when it virtually disappeared. Another de facto coup took place in Guinea-Bissau in 2010 when the military chief, loyal to the elected government, was overthrown in a mutiny. That coup is widely believed to have been orchestrated by suspected drug baron José Americo Bubo Na Tchuto, a former navy chief of staff who was operating out of the local UN office at the time.

Africans are noticing the democratic decay and they do not like it. Across 11 countries tracked by the Afrobarometer public opinion survey project—Botswana, Ghana, Lesotho, Malawi, Mali, Namibia, Nigeria, South Africa, Tanzania, Uganda, and Zambia—average satisfaction with democratic performance slipped by 5 percent (from 61 to 56 percent) between 1999 and 2008. There is a growing sense in Africa today that the democratic promises of the African renaissance are devolving in the same way that they did after independence. "The democratization process on the continent is not faring very well," Jean Ping, the Gabonese chairman of the African Union Commission, told *Newsweek* in July 2010. "The crises, they are repeating themselves."

Regionalism on Hold

The third leg of the African renaissance—strengthened regionalism aimed at building peace and raising Africa's role in global politics—has also faltered. The good governance-oriented African Union (AU), created in 2001, has been largely impotent aside from peacekeeping roles. Attempts to transform governance through peer pressure oriented initiatives, such as the African Peer Review Mechanism (APRM) under which countries agree to have their governance scrutinized by others, have created only incoherent bureaucracies, overblown

Nick Anderson Editorial Cartoon used with permission of Nick Anderson, the Washington Post Writers Group and the Cartoonist Group. All Rights Reserved.

rhetoric, and political games. In its first nine years, only 27 of the region's 48 countries have even accepted the APRM in principle, and of these only 14 have actually begun the process. The much-vaunted Pan-African Parliament, set up in 2004 as an advisory body to the AU, now holds just two brief meetings a year.

Meanwhile, plans for a regional free trade area and common currency made under the Abuja Treaty, signed by 51 sub-Saharan and North African countries at Abuja, Nigeria in 1991, are dead. "Once more Africa has drifted to the periphery, contrary to what we sought to achieve," former president Thabo Mbeki of South Africa said in May 2010.

Smaller regional initiatives are also stalled. The nine border-straddling "transfrontier parks" in southern Africa, aimed at boosting tourism and tourism-related investment by offering larger and more secure areas for sight-seeing, have gone nowhere. The 13,500 square mile Great Limpopo park, for instance, which lies along the South African-Mozambican-Zimbabwean border, has been dogged by poor infrastructure, mine-clearances, poaching, and population relocations. A $16 million German gift to get the park going now looks like a write-off; most travelers are staying on the South African side, and talk of 200,000 visitors a year has ended.

The number of armed conflicts waiting to happen in Africa has not changed either. Localized violence in the Niger River Delta is on the rise again as the amnesty for delta oil rebels there falls apart. Conflicts in Congo, Côte d'Ivoire, Guinea, Uganda, and Zimbabwe are all simmering. The UN High Commissioner for Refugees says there are 10 million refugees and internally displaced people in sub-Saharan Africa, double the number of a decade ago. State failure is increasingly an African phenomenon: 22 of the 37 states "on alert" in the *Foreign Policy Magazine*/Fund for Peace Failed States Index are in Africa.

A Victim of Vultures

As the hopes of the African renaissance have faded, vultures have moved in. In pursuit of natural resources and allies, China is gainfully buying off the region's governments who have lost their commitments to rights and democracy. Latin American drug barons, meanwhile, have exploited the same weaknesses to develop new trafficking routes to Europe. According to the UN, between $1 billion and $2 billion in cocaine is being trafficked through West Africa every year, up from virtually nothing ten years ago. Piracy off the Somali coast is in danger of spreading to the South African cape, according to maritime experts.

Developments on the ground have also been disappointing. In April 2010, Senegal's president Abdoulaye Wade unveiled a looming statue in Dakar called "The African Renaissance," a monstrosity of heroic, loin-clothed figures made by North Korean builders. The statue is supposed to represent the vigor of the African continent as it throws off the chains of colonialism (or "neocolonialism" according to the more exotic interpretations). The estimated costs of the monument, which Wade paid for by giving the North Koreans land that they subsequently sold, ranges from $28 to $70 million. If the United States were to spend a similar proportion of its national income (0.2 percent using the lower estimate) on such a statue, it would cost about $29 billion. Wade has asked the AU to declare the monument's date of unveiling as an annual African Renaissance Day. He has filed for a U.S. patent for the statue under his own name, as if billions of global citizens will buy trinkets of the monstrosity the way they do of the Statue of Liberty. More troublingly, Wade, elected in 2000, has manipulated the term limits of the 2001 constitution to extend his term and allow himself to run again in 2012.

Wade's statue symbolizes how little has changed in the last 20 years. Corruption, nepotism, mismanagement, and decay still abound. In 2005, *The Nambian* reported that a quotation from that country's former president Sam Nujoma, which was carved into the plinth of a similar statue built there by the same North Korean company in 2002, has since crumbled: "The 'S' of Sam is broken, the 'N' of Nujoma is gone altogether, and what was supposed to be 'motherland' is missing some of its letters, which are still hanging precariously from the remainder of the word." How long until Wade's statue—and the unfulfilled promise of the African renaissance that it represents—crumbles as well?

It is no wonder that world opinion has balked at calls for a new "big push" to pour resources into Africa, made most recently in former Prime Minister Tony Blair of the United Kingdom's 2005 Commission for Africa Report titled "Our Common Interest." G-7 [a group of seven industrialized nations] aid to sub-Saharan Africa is running at only $20–$30 billion a year, far less than the $40 billion promised at the group's 2005 Gleneagles summit. Gadfly aid critics from Africa, like Zambian economist Dambisa Moyo, now utter the previously unutterable: most aid to Africa should be stopped because it feeds dependency and corruption, contributing nothing to actual development. Donors have forgiven much debt—Africa's average external debt has fallen by half to 40 percent of GDP since 1996—but new infusions, both public and private, are drying up. [U2 singer and activist] Bono aside, aid to Africa is no longer chic.

African Governments Are Failing the People

Africa has had its share of bad luck to be sure. Global climate change, in the form of desertification and drought, is hitting the continent particularly hard. The tragedy of HIV/AIDS continues to claim one and a half million African lives a year, which is three-quarters of the global total, and has left 14 million orphans. But the domestic responses to these external shocks have been inadequate, especially when compared to those of other developing countries. The African Renaissance Coalition, a nongovernmental organization based in Lagos, [Nigeria,] chastised in June 2010 that African nations need to share the blame for their poor response to climate change: "A country like Nigeria, which is perhaps the largest contributor to climate change in Africa with its gas flaring, does not require or deserve the handouts from the West to stop this grossly anti-environmental activity." More broadly, blaming outside factors has never explained Africa's maladies.

The direct blame lies with corrupt leaders. Ironically, this is a bitter vindication of a key premise of the African renaissance, namely that bad leadership was at the heart of the region's postcolonial problems. Mandela's much-quoted words at the annual summit of the Organization of African Unity in 1994 have come back to haunt the region: "We must face the matter squarely that where there is something wrong in how we govern ourselves, it must be said that the fault is not in our stars but in ourselves, that we are ill-governed."

> "Trade liberalization has the greatest potential to help Africa emerge from poverty."

Africa Needs to Expand Free Trade

Marian L. Tupy

In the following viewpoint, Marian L. Tupy argues that Western nations need to abandon the belief that foreign aid can remedy Africa's problems. According to Tupy, aid has not ended widespread poverty in sub-Saharan Africa; only trade can do that. Tupy contends that expanding free trade by opening African markets to foreign goods will lead to greater competition from within Africa, boosting entrepreneurship and giving consumers more choice among competitively priced products. The author, however, notes that although African governments are enticed by free trade idealism, few have lowered tariffs to allow for equitable trade. She also chides Western governments for preaching trade liberalization while funding subsidies, holding on to some protective barriers of their own, and swamping the markets of developing nations with excess goods sold at prices low enough to undersell—and, in fact, destroy—competition from within those

Marian L. Tupy, "The False Promise of Gleneagles: Misguided Priorities at the Heart of the New Push for African Development," CATO Development Policy Analysis No. 9, April 24, 2009. Copyright © 2009 by CATO Institute. All rights reserved. Reproduced by permission.

nations. Tupy is a policy analyst at the Cato Institute's Center for Global Liberty and Prosperity.

As you read, consider the following questions:

1. According to Tupy, between 1975 and 2005, what was the annual gross domestic product (GDP) per capita growth rate in India? What was the growth rate in Africa?

2. Why does Tupy believe that World Bank structural adjustment loans to African nations may not be in those nations' best interests?

3. What is "agricultural dumping," as the author defines it?

In response to persisting poverty in Africa, representatives from the world's eight leading industrialized nations—Germany, Canada, the United States, France, Italy, Japan, the United Kingdom, and Russia [known as the G8]—met in Gleneagles, Scotland, in 2005 and agreed on a three-pronged approach to help Africa. They would increase foreign aid to the continent, reduce Africa's debt, and open their markets to African exports. Unfortunately, aid has harmed rather than helped Africa. It has failed to stimulate growth or reform, and encouraged waste and corruption. For example, aid has financed 40 percent of military spending in Africa. Similarly, debt relief has failed to prevent African countries from falling into debt again.

Trade liberalization has the greatest potential to help Africa emerge from poverty. Yet that is where the least amount of progress has been made. Negotiations on trade liberalization have ground to a halt, and the threat of protectionism looms large as the current global economic slowdown worsens.

The Gleneagles Summit, for all its good intentions, gave rise to unrealistic expectations. The heavy emphasis on aid and debt relief made Western actions appear to be chiefly responsible for poverty alleviation in Africa. In reality, the main obstacles to economic growth in Africa rest with Africa's policies and institutions, such as onerous business regulations and weak protection of property rights.

Africa remains the poorest and least economically free region on earth. The West should do all it can to help Africa integrate with the rest of the world. It should eliminate remaining restrictions on African exports and end Western farm subsidies. Africans, however, will have to make most of the changes needed to tackle African poverty.

Progress and Shortcomings

Sub-Saharan Africa (hereafter Africa) lags behind the rest of the world in most indicators of human well-being. Africans suffer from (among other afflictions) shorter life spans; higher rates of infant mortality; higher incidence of HIV/AIDS, malaria, and tuberculosis; and greater undernourishment than people do in other parts of the world.

Overall, Africa scored a mere 0.472 on the United Nations' 2006 Human Development Index, which is measured on a scale from 0 to 1, with higher values denoting higher standards of living. In comparison to Africa, the United States scored 0.948.

That is not to say that there have been no improvements in Africa over the last few decades. Between 1961 and 2002, for example, daily food supplies in terms of consumed calories increased in Africa from 2,055 to 2,207. Infant mortality declined from 177 per 1,000 live births between 1950 and 1955 to 101 in 2003. Life expectancy at birth rose from 37.4 years between 1950 and 1955 to 45.6 years in 2003.

Even so, according to data compiled by Angus Maddison of the University of Groningen, the income gap between Africa and other regions rose between 1960 and 2003. In 1960, an average Western European was 6.5 times richer than an average African. By 2003 that gap grew to 10.7 times. In 1960, an average African was slightly richer than an average inhabitant of Asia. By 2003, Asians were 2.4 times richer than Africans. . . .

Time to End Aid Dependency

The priorities set out by the G8, which put aid and debt relief ahead of trade, are misguided. Foreign aid to Africa has indeed increased and its debt was reduced, but little progress has been made on trade liberalization—the only agreement reached by the G8 that could lead to lasting economic improvements on the African continent.

Between 1975 and 2005, per capita aid to Africa averaged $24.60 per year. By contrast, in China it averaged $1.50 and in India $2. Over the same time period, the compounded average annual GDP [gross domestic product] growth rate per capita in China was 7.9 percent and in India 3.5 percent. In Africa it was a negative 0.16 percent.

The importance of growth cannot be overemphasized. There is not a single example of a country emerging from widespread poverty without sustained economic growth. As University of Oxford professor Paul Collier writes, "Growth is not a cure-all, but lack of growth is a kill-all." Growth cannot solve all problems in the developing world, but without growth there can be no lasting solution to the challenges faced by developing countries.

Thus, Martin Ravallion and Shaohua Chen of the World Bank write, between 1981 and 2005, the number of people with an income below $1.25 per day in China declined from 84 percent to 15.9 percent, reducing the absolute number of poor from 835.1 million to 207.7 million. In India, poverty declined from 59.8 percent to 41.6 percent. (Because of population growth, however, the number of poor rose from 420.5 million to 455.8 million.) In Africa, the poverty rate declined slightly from 53.7 percent to 51.2 percent. As in India, population growth increased the absolute number of poor from 213.7 million to 390.6 million.

The failure of foreign aid to improve growth rates in Africa has not stood in the way of those who want to see more of it. In 2005, for example, Columbia University professor Jeffrey Sachs unveiled his plan to end extreme poverty around the world by 2025. Rich countries, Sachs argued, should commit themselves to increasing annual aid to the world's poorest nations from $74 billion in 2006 to $135 billion in 2015. Also in 2005, the Commission for Africa called for doubling aid to Africa to $50 billion by 2010 and tripling it to $75 billion by 2015. In the end, the G8 committed itself to doubling aid to Africa to $50 billion per year.

Discarding Old Paradigms

In the 1950s and 1960s, many development economists believed in the "vicious cycle of poverty" theory, which argued that poverty in the developing world prevented the accumulation of domestic savings (i.e., people in poor countries consumed all of their income and had nothing left to save and invest). Low savings resulted in low domestic investment, and low investment was seen as the main impediment to rapid economic growth. Foreign aid, therefore, was intended to fill the apparent gap between insufficient savings and the requisite investment in the economy. Today's calls for more foreign aid are based largely on the same theory.

Yet experience contradicts the "vicious cycle of poverty" theory. Today, many formerly poor countries enjoy high standards of living, while others have stagnated or, in some cases, regressed. For example, the 1960 per capita income in South Korea was $1,226. In Ghana it was $1,378. By 2003 South Korea had reached $15,732, while Ghana had fallen to $1,360. As New York University professor William Easterly writes, "It doesn't help the poverty trap story that 11 out of the 28 poorest countries in 1985 had not been in the poorest fifth back in 1950. They had gotten into poverty by declining from above, rather than being stuck in it from below, while others escaped. If the identity of who is in the poverty trap keeps changing, it must not be much of a trap."

Countries that improve their policies and institutions—by increasing their trade openness, limiting state intervention in the economy, building a business-friendly environment, and emphasizing protection of property rights and the rule of law—tend to grow faster than others. Such countries also tend to attract foreign capital, which can help to increase economic growth. Improvement in policies and institutions also creates a suitable environment for growth in domestic investment. As trust in institutions such as the rule of law and protection of private property grows, people feel more confident investing in the local economy.

Today, the size and the scope of global capital markets make Africa's access to capital potentially easier than at any time in the past. Indeed, private capital flows to developing countries now dwarfs aid flows. According to Adam Lerrick of the American Enterprise Institute, "The development banks now supply a mere 2 percent of the average net [capital worth] $200 billion that the capital markets provide."

Aid Has Not Led to Economic Reform

Sub-Saharan Africa is the least economically free region in the world. There is a general consensus among economists that Africa needs to catch up with the rest of the world in terms of economic liberalization. Aid is often intended to promote policy reform, yet it has helped to create disincentives to liberalization for a number of reasons.

For example, aid is often driven by foreign policy considerations, not economics. For much of the Cold War, African countries were given bilateral and multilateral assistance on the basis of their geopolitical importance to the West and the

Soviet Union. As recent American aid to Ethiopia and Chinese aid to Sudan show, geopolitical interests continue to influence aid decisions today.

Aid has not led to economic reforms in Africa. In the 1980s, the World Bank started to promote structural adjustment loans that were meant to disburse aid to countries in exchange for their commitment to economic reforms. Such conditional lending soon proved ineffective, in part because aid agencies have no enforcement mechanism, and also because they have a well-known bureaucratic incentive to lend, which undermines the credibility of their conditionality.

In fact, aid may also actively retard policy reform. Between 1970 and 1993, for example, the World Bank and the IMF [International Monetary Fund] gave Zambia 18 adjustment loans with little or no reforms taking place, forcing World Bank researchers to conclude that "this large amount of assistance sustained a poor policy regime." More generally, two World Bank researchers concluded that "higher aid slowed reform [in the developing world] over the 1980–2000 period."

Even in those countries that follow sensible macroeconomic policies, aid appears to have no positive effect and may go so far as to discourage reform. Some World Bank research claimed that developing countries that follow good fiscal, monetary, and trade policies benefit from foreign aid. But that research has been difficult to independently corroborate. Scholars who used updated World Bank data found no positive correlation between foreign aid and economic growth in countries with "good policies." Research suggests that when governments do decide to undertake economic reforms, they tend to do so because of domestic factors, including economic crises. . . .

The Benefits of Trade Liberalization

The theoretical benefits of trade are well known. Trade improves global efficiency in resource allocation or, to put it dif-

The West Must Drop Trade Barriers

Trade barriers that deny African products and services access to Western markets are not only blatantly unfair, they are an assault on the human rights of the African people. When African producers are denied access to Western markets, they are being denied access to a livelihood, to providing for their families and communities. Eliminating these barriers is not just a prerequisite to addressing the need for fair competition, but key to removing a fundamental impediment that has denied Africa the same economic empowerment opportunities the West has enjoyed for a long time. These barriers have made African economies mainly exporters of raw primary commodities and importers of value-added finished products from the West. It is fair to say that the continent has been consigned to being producers of what they do not consume and consumers of what they do not produce.

Andrew Rogasira, interviewed by the
Journal of International Affairs, *Spring/Summer 2009.*

ferently, it provides a superior way of delivering goods and services to those who value them most. An expanded market allows traders to gain from specializing in the production of those goods and services that they do best (i.e., the law of comparative advantage). Trade allows consumers to benefit from more-efficient methods of production. Without large markets for goods and services, it would not be economical to separate production into specific operations and plan large production runs. Large production runs, in turn, are instrumental to reducing the cost of a product. The reduction of the cost of production leads to cheaper goods and services, which increases the real standard of living.

But what does research say about actual benefits to Africa from trade liberalization? In a much-cited 2005 paper, World Bank researchers estimated African benefits from trade liberalization. According to the World Bank, "The results suggest moving to free global merchandise trade would boost real incomes in sub-Saharan Africa proportionately more than in other developing countries or in high-income countries, despite a terms of trade loss in parts of the region. Farm employment and output, the real value of agricultural and food exports, the real returns to farm land and unskilled labor, and real net farm incomes would all rise in the region, thereby alleviating poverty."

In real terms, annual welfare in Africa would be $4.8 billion greater in 2015 than would be the case had no liberalization taken place. There would be growth in agricultural incomes and in employment. Moreover, Africa stands to gain much from internal trade liberalization. Denis Medvedev of the World Bank has estimated that by 2015, annual welfare gains from intra-African trade liberalization would amount to 36 percent of all the welfare gains that Africa stands to receive from global trade liberalization.

Protectionist Policies Need to End

The case against developed world protectionism against products from developing countries, including Africa, is well known. Seventy-three percent of poor people in developing countries live in rural areas and 60 percent of the labor force in low-income countries derives its income from agriculture. Agriculture and agro-related services generate 25 percent of low-income countries' GDP.

Yet, the developed world's protection against the developing world's agricultural exports is four to seven times higher than that on the developing world's manufacturing exports. Many agricultural goods from Africa and other developing countries face tariff escalation. Tariffs of up to 500 percent are sometimes applied by the United States, European Union, Japan, and Canada on products that include beef, dairy products, vegetables, fresh fruit, cereals, sugar, prepared fruit and vegetables, wine, spirits, and tobacco.

Rich countries' support for agriculture undercuts competition from cheaper products originating in the developing world. In 2007, agricultural support in the countries of the Organization for Economic Cooperation and Development came to about $365 billion. Agricultural subsidies in rich countries also cause overproduction of certain farm products. That agricultural surplus is often dumped on the world markets, which depresses prices and undermines farmers in poor countries. Agricultural dumping is an especially serious problem for many developing countries, where agricultural production enjoys a comparative advantage over the developed world. The European Union's Common Agricultural Policy alone is estimated to cause $20 billion worth of annual losses in poor countries.

In short, because agriculture is such an important part of developing countries' economies, and because it receives extensive protection in developed countries, such protectionism undermines markets and makes the developed world's proclamations in favor of free trade sound hollow and hypocritical.

African Protectionism

Unfortunately, when it comes to trade protectionism, Africa is far from blameless. In fact, Africa is one of the world's most protectionist regions. Average applied tariff rates in Africa, for example, remain comparatively high. Whereas average applied tariffs in high-income Organization for Economic Co-operation and Development countries fell from 9.5 percent to 2.9 percent between 1988 and 2007 (a 70 percent reduction), average applied tariffs in Africa only fell from 26.6 percent to 13.1 percent between 1987 and 2007 (a 50 percent reduction).

In addition to tariffs, there is a plethora of nontariff barriers to trade that African countries employ. According to the Commission for Africa, "the costs and difficulty of moving goods across, between, in and out of some African countries can be far higher than in richer countries, undermining Africa's competitiveness. . . . In the 1990s, it cost about the same to clear a 20-foot container through ports of Abidjan or Dakar as it did to ship the same container all the way to a north-European port. Sub-Saharan Africa suffers from the highest average customs delays in the world: for example, Estonia and Lithuania require only one day for customs clearance—versus 30 days on average for Ethiopia."

African countries also impose significantly higher tariffs on one another than rich countries impose on Africa. The World Bank data show that African countries levy an average applied tariff of 34 percent on agricultural exports from other African countries. Industrial countries, by contrast, levy an average applied tariff of 24 percent on African agricultural exports. Similarly, African countries maintain an average applied tariff of 21 percent on non-agricultural exports from other African countries. Industrial countries maintain an average applied tariff of 4 percent on African non-agricultural exports.

Not surprisingly, African intraregional trade covered only 10 percent of African exports. In contrast, 68 percent of exports from countries in Western Europe were exported to other Western European countries. Similarly, 40 percent of North American exports were to other countries in North America.

The Failure of Doha

At the conclusion of the Gleneagles summit, [then British prime minister] Tony Blair described the successful conclusion of the Doha Round of negotiations on trade as "a necessary element of our [G8] work to reduce global poverty." The negotiations launched in [Doha] Qatar in 2001 were dubbed the "Doha Development Agenda," so as to highlight that the greatest beneficiaries of future trade liberalization would be developing countries, including African countries. Unfortunately, Doha became the first round of negotiations on trade liberalization in the post–World War II era that ended in failure.

Many countries deserve blame for the failure of the Doha round. The Europeans failed to agree to deeper cuts in agricultural tariffs. Americans failed to agree to real cuts in farm subsidies. The Indians and the Brazilians failed to move sufficiently on liberalization of their manufacturing sectors. But one of the most destructive and certainly the most self-defeating roles in bringing about the collapse of negotiations was played by the African delegates.

The Doha round of negotiations on trade liberalization ran into trouble during the 2003 ministerial meeting in Cancun. Egged on by Oxfam, African and other developing countries demanded that they be exempted from further commitments to trade liberalization. As far as the African countries were concerned, trade liberalization was a one-way street: the developed world would open its markets to African goods, while Africa would continue to shut goods made in the developed world out of African markets.

Economic theory and empirical evidence shows that there is much wisdom in unilateral liberalization, and developing countries gain enormously from opening their markets to foreign imports irrespective of what other countries do. But unilateral liberalization was not on the table in Cancun. Global negotiations on trade liberalization happen along long-established mercantilist lines, where countries trade "concessions" on "market access" with one another.

At the heart of this mercantilist view of trade is a deep misunderstanding of the role that foreign competition plays in stimulating domestic production. Mercantilists see imports as a threat, which is why, at Cancun, African trade ministers emphasized exports and access to developed world markets, as opposed to opening their own countries to foreign goods. In reality, imports increase competition and specialization, and increased specialization leads to increased productivity. In a competitive market, reduction of the cost of production then leads to cheaper goods and services, which in turn increases the real standard of living. That is a major reason why people living in more open economies tend to be richer.

The Cancun meeting collapsed around a minor issue of trade facilitation. The refusal of developing countries, including African states, to negotiate about the streamlining of the paperwork needed to clear imports at the border convinced the Mexican chairman of the conference that there was no point in discussing the much more contentious issue of tariff reductions. With the battle lines drawn at Cancun, all sides were determined to hold out for the best possible deal—which was supposed to be struck at the next ministerial meeting in Hong Kong in December of 2005. But that deal was never struck, as the meeting in Hong Kong made little headway.

Doha's failure is a tragedy for Africa. Trade liberalization is, after all, most advantageous to the most protectionist countries and Africa remains one of the most protectionist regions in the world. True, Africans were never going to get everything that they wanted. It is also true that the Doha round exposed the basic hypocrisy of the developed countries that preach free trade, but continue to insist on protecting the "sensitive" sectors of their economies, like agriculture.

Reaching an agreement would have been a step in the right direction. Not only would it allow Africans greater access to developed world markets than they currently enjoy, but it would also allow Africans to "lock in" those new market access "gains" without the fear of backsliding by some WTO [World Trade Organization] member states. Similarly, it would lock in Africa's own commitments, making a return to protectionism more difficult. Importantly, it would allow the African states to use the WTO adjudication mechanisms to hold other member states, including other African countries, true to their trade liberalization commitments. The WTO's dispute resolution process has already proven to be a very effective mechanism for small developing countries to force change in the trade policies of large developed nations. The above considerations are especially important now that the world economy has entered a slowdown and fears of protectionism abound.

| "Over the past two decades, sub-Saharan Africa has lost $272 billion from the effects of trade liberalisation."

Free Trade Is Devastating African Economies

Gregory Elich

In the following viewpoint, Gregory Elich claims that free trade has devastated the economies of developing African nations. In his view, Western powers have imposed free trade on developing nations in order to open markets and remove protectionist barriers to a host of imports. The flood of foreign goods has swamped local African economies, Elich contends, forcing many in the agricultural, fishing, and burgeoning industrial fields to close up shop because they cannot compete with the cheap foods and products imported from foreign economic giants. Elich claims the United States and international lending agencies are so determined to force free trade on Africa that they withhold aid from needy countries unless those countries accept the removal of tariffs and agree to open their markets to ruinous foreign competition. Without recourse, these developing nations are compelled to comply and thus suffer the damage that undermines economic growth and destroys livelihoods. Author of Strange Liberation:

Militarism, Mayhem, and the Pursuit of Profit, *Gregory Elich is a writer focusing on globalization issues.*

As you read, consider the following questions:

1. According to Elich, Ghana once manufactured enough tomato paste for its needs, but now the author states that Ghana imports what percentage of its tomato paste supply?

2. As Elich reports, the threefold rise in poultry imports to Cameroon led to a loss of how many domestic poultry jobs?

3. According to Christian Aid, how much money has sub-Saharan Africa lost since 1990 due to the impact of trade liberalization?

So often we are told that the free market is the path to economic prosperity. All an impoverished nation needs to do is privatise, deregulate, reduce the size and role of government, cut tariff protections and open its economy to foreign investors, and it too can become a developed model economy. This gospel is preached by the US and Western European nations and enforced through international financial institutions such as the IMF [International Monetary Fund], World Bank and the World Trade Organisation (WTO).

The neoliberal economic model, it is claimed, is beneficial for all nations and in all circumstances. But is it true? These assertions never acknowledge the actual experience of developing nations that implement these policies. To do so would dispel such notions. The effect of free trade on agricultural development in sub-Saharan Africa provides a characteristic example.

Drying Up Domestic Agricultural Markets

Ghana faithfully enacted structural adjustment programmes in the 1990s in accordance with agreements it had signed with the IMF and World Bank. Subsidies to farmers were ended and the state-run seed company was closed down. The removal of subsidies caused the price of fertiliser to skyrocket, with a predictable fall in consumption and its consequent effect on agricultural production levels.

Government programmes that actively supported farmers were ended, and loans by commercial banks to agricultural producers nearly dried up. Import tariffs were dramatically reduced and in many cases eliminated altogether. This led to a flood of cheap imports from abroad. Domestic smallholders were compelled to compete with imports from subsidised large-scale Western agribusinesses.

In the US, Western Europe and Japan, many billions of dollars are provided to rice growers each year, allowing them to set an export price at well below the cost of production. Local growers in sub-Saharan Africa simply cannot compete on equal terms, especially as they must manage without subsidies due to IMF/World Bank strictures.

Such "free market competition" has brought only hardship to Ghanaian farmers. Surveys in 2002 and 2004 found that two-thirds of rice growers in Ghana operated at a loss. "Why are we suffering?", a Ghanaian farmer asked. "Maybe the international lenders want us to be totally dependent on them."

Closing Canneries and Processing Plants

Heavily subsidised tomato paste imports from the US and Western Europe into Ghana increased by more than five times in the decade ending in 2002. The wholesale closure of domestic tomato processing plants and storage facilities resulted, hampering the prospects of success for growers. On top of that, many plants were forced to shut down due to IMF-imposed structural adjustment plans. Offered for privatisation, these plants in many cases found no buyers, and thus had to cease operations in accordance with neoliberal principles.

One farmer commented on the local cannery in his area, which had "made things easier for us". But now it is closed. As a state-run firm, it was no longer allowed to operate without a buyer. "Selling our tomatoes is a game of chance," he said. "It's heartbreaking to stand here and watch the fruit go rotten."

Not surprisingly, given such factors, imports now account for 90% of the tomato paste sold in Ghana, leading the King of Asante, Otumfuo Osei Tutu II to comment recently: "We used to grow enough tomatoes here for our needs. We even used to have a tomato-canning factory in the north [of the country]! Today we import tomato paste from wherever. Why? Why are we importing everything? You cannot be a mighty country or continent lying in bed and importing everything."

The Glut of Imports

In Senegal, import levels of tomato paste have increased by a factor of 15 times, leading to a halving of local production. Throughout sub-Saharan Africa similar patterns are developing.

Poultry imports into Ghana have increased so much that many domestic farms are having to slaughter thousands of chickens a week due to market saturation. Hatcheries are operating at under half of their capacity. In Senegal, poultry imports over the six-year period ending in 2002 increased by a factor of 33 times, causing 40% of poultry farmers to go out of business.

Under WTO agreements, Ghana is permitted to raise the tariff on poultry to as high as 99%. But when the nation actually attempted to raise its tariff from 20% to 45%, the IMF threatened to halt future loan disbursements and the tariff increase was never put into effect.

Kenneth Quartey, owner of one of the largest poultry farms in Ghana, has had to slash operations and reduce staff due to competition from imports. "What you're breeding is a culture of dependency," he pointed out.

No Hope in Free Trade

Globalisation has transformed states in Africa, and reduced their economic and political independence. For neoliberal globalisation builds the growth and development of one part of the world on the back of other parts. That is done through the *idea* of a global free market, yet we know that the most basic feature of neoliberalism is the systematic use of state power to impose market imperatives through a domestic process that is replicated internationally. Part of Africa's difficulty is thus countering the intellectual deceit peddled by international financial institutions—that globalisation brings universal economic growth rather than a continued subordination to the rule of capital. Globalisation brings poverty and inequality to Africa as a result of the continent's uneven incorporation into the world economy. The main hope for the future is not free trade, open markets and technological gains; rather, it is resistance to the impact of globalisation by workers and peasants, and the construction by Africans themselves of an alternative future.

Roy Bush,
Soundings, *Summer 2008.*

Ruining Livelihoods

Liberalisation has also had a devastating effect on the fishing industry in Ghana. European commercial fishing vessels operate on a large-scale level of production, and are able to sell their produce at much lower prices than local fishermen can manage.

Furthermore, with their deep drafts and large nets, these commercial fishing vessels often inadvertently drag along the nets and traps used by local fishermen, wiping out their production. With declining income and growing debt, many domestic fishermen have been forced to abandon fishing altogether.

In Cameroon, a threefold increase in poultry imports over a five-year period reduced local production and led to the loss of over 100,000 rural jobs every year. It took only five years to drive 92% of poultry farmers out of business. In Mozambique, vegetable oil imports now account for 81% of the total market, while most oil-crushing operations have closed.

Economic restructuring in Côte d'Ivoire transformed agriculture. By the turn of the century, the 10 rice mills that had been built by the state-owned rice company were privatised. Two years later, not one remained in business. Inevitably, the privatisation drive closed down the rice company. Also eliminated were fertiliser subsidies for rice growers, state-owned seed farms and price supports for locally produced rice. In their place there was only the removal of restrictions on imports.

Aid with Strings Attached

Aid is regarded among the Western public as an act of selfless beneficence. Yet aid almost always comes with strings attached, in ways that align with neoliberal goals. The US Millennium Challenge Account [a foreign aid agency that disburses aid to countries demonstrating good governance policies] is helping to fund agricultural modernisation in Ghana for selected crops, none of which compete with US exports. Rice is specifically excluded from the grant.

Furthermore, for a nation to receive money from the account it must rank high in so-called "economic freedom". That is, it must demonstrate that it is implementing neoliberal policies and opening its economy to Western corporate interests.

The provision of food aid offers an opportunity for ideological and commercial penetration. The US Department of

Agriculture (USDA) is rather blunt about its objectives when it comes to food aid. Although it is generally cheaper, quicker and more efficient to send money to a recipient nation for the purchase of regionally produced food, the US will only provide direct shipments of its own food.

Among the various food aid programmes, the USDA reports, Public Law 480 "seeks to expand foreign markets for US agricultural products, combat hunger and encourage economic development in developing countries." Note which goal is listed first. Recipient nations under the Title I option of the programme are required to "have the potential to become commercial markets for US agricultural commodities".

Using Aid to Flood Africa with US Goods

The US Food for Progress Programme provides "for the donation or credit sale of US commodities" in order to "support democracy and an expansion of private enterprise". Under this programme, food is given to "private voluntary organisations to introduce elements of free enterprise into the countries' agricultural economies".

USDA reports proudly that the programme has never funded recipient nations to purchase food from regional sources. All of the food aid programmes and agricultural trade programmes "are designed to develop and expand commercial outlets for US commodities in world markets". Aid is provided where it can advance the interests of US agribusiness. Humanitarian concerns play a secondary role, when they factor at all.

The African Growth and Opportunities Act (AGOA) was initially designed to primarily benefit US textile producers wanting to take advantage of cheap labour in sub-Saharan Africa.

The Act offers the prospect of expanded trade with African countries that the US designates as having "market-based economies" that have eliminated "barriers to US trade and investment". As it has turned out, petroleum exports from Nigeria and Angola to the US predominate, accounting for 85% of exports under AGOA.

US technical assistance under AGOA is provided only to those nations that meet certain conditions. They must liberalise trade, harmonise their laws and regulations with the WTO, carry out financial restructuring, and promote increased agribusiness "linkages".

Efforts are unceasing to further expose the African market to Western penetration. In 2007, African nations were obliged by the WTO to open 80% of their markets to European imports. The World Bank's International Finance Corporation actively works to promote the easing of restrictions on imports from Western nations and for what it terms "improving the business environment". Improvement, it goes without saying, is in the eyes of Western investors.

Forcing Liberalization of Africa

The US Agency for International Development (USAID) launched the African Global Competitiveness Initiative in 2006. This programme seeks ways to remove "barriers to investment" and to carry out "practical solutions" leading to "a more competitive environment for investment and trade". Competition, as always, is on unequal terms. Protections are to be removed, and one of the key components of the initiative is recommending to African nations that they change "tariff and non-tariff barriers" and "regulatory requirements."

Political meddling goes hand in hand with these efforts. "Where change is slow," USAID explains, "support to reform-oriented leaders—in both the public and private sectors—to press for change can help galvanise the needed internal political will."

Another of USAID's programmes is Trade for African Development and Enterprise, which supports trade "reform" and "investment in and privatisation of African enterprise". Among its achievements, USAID "assisted the privatisation of the seed industry" in Ghana, an action that had harsh results for domestic farmers.

USAID also initiated the South African Agriculture Financial Restructuring and Privatisation Programme (SARPP), which extended privatisation efforts to include "restructuring of agricultural assets and enterprises" in South Africa. The SARPP approach to land reform is the "willing buyer/willing seller" model, which has quite effectively stalled any meaningful progress.

Agriculture is of primary importance to the economies of sub-Saharan Africa. Free trade and free market policies have brought only hardship. "Interestingly, in the countries where they subsidise, only about 5% of the population are farmers," comments the National Union of Cotton Farmers of Burkina Faso. "Here, farmers represent some 80% of a population that is becoming increasingly impoverished on land that is itself becoming poorer, without the least help from the state."

Christian Aid calculates that over the past two decades, sub-Saharan Africa has lost $272 billion from the effects of trade liberalisation. That money did not vanish. It is being transferred to wealthy corporate pockets in the developed nations.

It is worth noting that none of the developed nations achieved their economic status through free trade policies. Protectionist measures were essential for development. And nations such as South Korea that managed to successfully leap from developing conditions to developed economies did so through policies that ran counter to free market principles.

The free market mantra, as spouted by the West, is self-serving. It is only Western corporate interests that gain from neo-liberal orthodoxies, which bring only privation to the many. What is needed is fair trade, not free trade.

> "Healthcare delivery in Africa is never going to improve ... while it remains under the control of [the] public sector."

Health Care in Africa Has Not Improved

Thompson Ayodele

In the following viewpoint, Thompson Ayodele maintains that foreign aid money to improve health care in African nations is not reaching patients or health care services. Ayodele claims that both government officials and health care operators are siphoning off money from these funds for personal gain. Whatever aid does reach hospitals, clinics, or pharmacies is therefore insufficient to help the sick, the author contends. Ayodele calls upon donor nations and international charities to stop routing funds through African governments and, instead, bolster private health care institutions that rely on competition and accountability to improve their patient services. Ayodele is executive director of the Initiative for Public Policy Analysis, a think tank based in Lagos, Nigeria.

As you read, consider the following questions:

1. Citing World Health Organization statistics, Ayodele states that what percentage of Africans lack access to essential medicines?

2. According to the author, why do many publicly funded drugs never reach hospitals or other care centers?

3. What are the three reasons Ayodele gives to support his assertion that funding private health care in Africa would improve services?

After decades of neglect, the provision of effective health-care is becoming one of the biggest concerns in Africa. Both foreign donors and African governments are keen to make this their priority, and consequently the money taps have been opened. Foreign aid in the form of hard currency is flowing in unprecedented quantities into the ministries of health of many African countries. Despite this generosity, however, things are not really improving on the ground: medical staff are demoralised, access to essential medicines remains low, and corruption remains a serious problem.

The Development Assistance for Health (DAH) [an international fund] has increased from US$2.5 billion in 1990 to over US$13 billion in 2005. Overall, approximately ten percent of Africa's health care expenditure is now financed directly by donor aid. Nevertheless, the majority of African countries are way off-track with their progress towards the health-related Millennium Development Goals.

Health Care Shortfalls and Transparency

Access to essential medicines remains low in the poorest parts in the world. According to the World Health Organisation, over 50 per cent of Africans lack access to essential medicines. Around the world, over 10 million children in developing countries die unnecessarily from diseases that are easily preventable and cheap to treat, such as diarrhoea, measles and malaria. Furthermore, up to 80 per cent of Africans have to pay for treatment straight from their own pockets. In short, public health systems are failing to deliver.

A major factor behind this failure of foreign aid to improve healthcare is the fact that nearly all of it first passes through health ministries before it can reach patients. According to studies undertaken by the World Health Organization and the Center for Global Development in Washington DC, bureaucrats have little idea of what actually happens to the money after it is handed over to the government.

As a result of these lax controls, a great deal of this money is subverted by health officials for private gain, particularly in countries that have a problem with corruption. This can occur in the ministry itself, or further down the line in the hospital. A study by Maureen Lewis of the World Bank shows how corruption in the health care sector of developing countries is so bad that it is severely undermining the effectiveness of donor funding.

The leakage of drugs from the supply chain is a particular problem, mainly because publicly funded drugs can fetch a high price if stolen and resold on the black market. Recent surveys in Nigeria show that 28 public health centres had received no drugs from the federal government in two years. Meanwhile, a 2001 study by the World Bank showed that fewer than half of government health facilities in Lagos and Kogi states had received drugs from the federal government.

Last year [2007], NAFDAC [National Agency for Food and Drug Administration and Control in Nigeria] boss Dora Akunyili disclosed that it is commonplace for donated drugs such as Vitamin A capsules, Mectizan and Coartem tablets and oral rehydration salt to be pilfered and re-sold on the open market. In the same vein, it was reported that Global Fund was considering suspending two of Nigeria's five-year grants totaling $80 million because of concerns over grant management,

Too Few Health Care Workers

Recently, considerable attention has been focused on the apparent shortage of health workers in countries with the poorest health indicators. . . . According to recent WHO [World Health Organization] estimates, the current workforce in some of the most affected countries in sub-Saharan Africa would need to be scaled up by as much as 140% to attain international health development targets such as those in the Millennium Declaration. The problem is so serious that in many instances there is simply not enough human capacity even to absorb, deploy and efficiently use the substantial additional funds that are considered necessary to improve health in these countries.

Yohannes Kinfu et al.,
Bulletin of the World Health Organization, *2009.*

transparency of fund allocation and grant implementation and the ability of the Nigerian government to achieve the goals of the grants. The Global Fund has already terminated grants to Uganda and Chad.

And this is not counting the dozens of other forms of corruption that plague the health system in Nigeria, including mismanagement of funds at the ministry and hospital level; absenteeism; staff extracting payments from patients for services that are supposed to be free; and the abuse of procurement contracts for hospital supplies.

According to the NGO [nongovernmental organization] Human Rights Watch 'the government's failure to tackle local-level corruption violates Nigeria's obligation to provide basic health and education services to its citizens.'

End Government Control of Health Care

Add to this the chronic mismanagement that has left health workers owed months' pay and hospitals with obsolete equipment, and it is seems hardly surprising that donor funding is not making much of a difference to patients' health.

Healthcare delivery in Africa is never going to improve, however, while it remains under the control of [the] public sector. Government ministries have very few incentives to deliver care to patients other than the goodwill of their staff. As any manager of a private company will tell you, relying on this alone is not going to keep your customers. Unless there is a significant change in the way we manage the health sector, there will be few improvements—no matter how much money donors spend.

Bearing in mind the historic failure of African public health systems to provide citizens with the care they deserve, we should shift towards a situation in which governments no longer provide and manage all healthcare. The private sector should be given a far bigger role as well.

The advantages of this are three-fold. In the first place it would reduce corruption. Corruption certainly also exists in the private sector, but any private enterprise that has not shown integrity risks being excluded from future programmes and contracts. Secondly, since private businesses care deeply about their reputation, there would be pressure to deliver whatever it sets out to accomplish. After all, without reputation, there are no customers, and therefore no business. Thirdly, putting private sector bodies into competition with each other would force them to improve their productivity and improve patient care. Costs would fall and standards would rise. The opposite happens in the public sector, where there are few incentives to improve ways of working, and operations are disrupted the moment there is a change of government or ministers.

According to the International Finance Corporation, 60 per cent of the $16.7bn [billion] spent on health in Africa in 2005 was privately financed, with half of that money being spent in the private sector. It is time to harness this huge amount of capacity so it can work for patients in an efficient and equitable way.

It has been demonstrated by various health departments in Africa that most of the funds granted for disease prevention or control are largely misused. Grant-makers must let the private sector be the foundation upon which efficient and durable healthcare delivery will be built. To do otherwise would be to condemn millions more patients to an early death.

"All over Africa, individual entrepreneurs and local businesses are making small but significant steps in a positive direction."

Africa Is Making Strides in Sustainable Entrepreneurship

Helene Gallis

In the following viewpoint, Helene Gallis sees opportunities in various sustainable business practices in Africa. She believes that Africa's new entrepreneurs—who are forced to generate innovative business models based on lack of energy, irrigation, industrial machinery, and other technologies in short supply—are creating products and services with a low ecological impact. Gallis praises these businesspeople and suggests that much of the developed world could learn sustainable, community-oriented strategies from them that would serve future economies well in a world that may soon run short of oil, fossil-fuel-based electricity, and low-cost transportation. Helene Gallis is a writer and former intern at the Worldwatch Institute, a sustainable development organization.

Helene Gallis, "Sustainable Entrepreneurship in Africa," *World Watch*, vol. 23, no. 4, July/August 2010. Worldwatch Institute, Copyright 2010. www.worldwatch.org. Reproduced by permission.

As you read, consider the following questions:

1. What are the factors that define the "triple bottom line" thinking that Gallis says African entrepreneurs must employ to be successful?

2. What is M-Pesa, as Gallis defines it?

3. What does the author see as the advantages of "heirloom design" in Africa?

William Kamkwamba became an African entrepreneurship superstar when international media caught on to his exceptional engineering skills. In 2001, only 14 years old and with limited formal schooling, he managed to build a fully functioning windmill to provide his family with electricity, basing the construction on pictures found in books at the local library and using mainly scrap metal and wood. The Malawi native later drew international attention as a speaker at the inspiring online TED [Technology Entertainment Design] conferences, which led in turn to a coauthored bestselling book on his life and achievements (*The Boy Who Harnessed the Wind*). And he's still not coasting: William continues inventing and fundraising for various projects in his home village.

A Unique Story

William Kamkwamba's story is uniquely inspiring. He stakes out a path that hopefully many will follow, both in developing and in developed countries. Most importantly, he represents an image of Africa and Africans that rejects the pity and guilt commonly invoked by most news stories out of the continent. In fact, he represents the opposite—and may simultaneously be offering solutions to poverty, degradation, starvation, aid dependency, and corruption.

But exactly how many clever entrepreneurs like him might it take to address the development needs of Africa, and would it even be ecologically possible? This question of scaleability is so important that it is worth looking into. William's fame—his NGO [nongovernmental organization], his blog, sales of his book, plus a documentary due later this year [2010]—has generated funds to provide his village with wind and solar power, irrigation equipment for agriculture, malaria nets, improved sanitation, and wells for drinking water, among other things. Indeed, many of the development needs of the village's 60 families have been addressed.

However, these fantastic achievements remain drops in a vast ocean when looking at the country as a whole, not to mention the entire continent. Malawi's development challenges are immense. Forty percent of the population of 13 million live in poverty; 20 percent of children under the age of five are undernourished; adult illiteracy is nearly 30 percent; and an estimated 1 million are HIV-positive, to name a few. If the country only had a brigade of, say, 10,000 innovators and entrepreneurs just like William Kamkwamba who were equally successful at fundraising, Malawi's problems might be solved.

Focusing on Sustainability

The phrase "sustainable entrepreneurship" evokes a lot and little at the same time. Sustainability has become such an overused term that it barely has any concrete meaning anymore. Entrepreneurship is a bit clearer: We envision a successful businessman owning his or her own company and achieving economic success through sacrificing blood, sweat, and tears. The fact that the term entrepreneurship is so closely related to conventional economic measures of success hints at how difficult it might be to combine the idea with true social and environmental responsibility. Entrepreneurship in its current meaning is a product of our current cultural paradigm, which holds that economic growth (measured nationally by GDP [gross domestic product]) is a sign of success and consumerism equates with wellbeing.

Efforts to spread sustainable entrepreneurship in developing countries (such as the train-the-trainer workshop "Smart Start-up: Sustainable Entrepreneurship in Africa," co-organized by the Swedish Government and the UNEP [United Nations Environment Programme]/Wuppertal Institute Centre for Cleaner Production and Consumption in April [2010]) focus on "triple bottom line" thinking. For an entrepreneur to be successful, he or she must take into consideration social, environmental, and economic factors in equal measure. However, training materials on sustainable entrepreneurship still mainly stress the potential for making a fortune, rather than on helping to heal the planet or contributing to non-monetary wealth of communities.

In addition, social entrepreneurship organizations, networks, and funders have accumulated lots of related experiences over the last few years, but they still need to incorporate a deeper ecological understanding of working within planetary limits. The main difference in these approaches is the emphasis environmental concerns are given. Michael Vollman of the social entrepreneurship organization Ashoka explains that, in their terminology, environmental work is one of six areas within which social entrepreneurship projects are carried out, as opposed to an over-arching theme in sustainable entrepreneurship.

And that means, in turn, that another trail must be blazed—perhaps the trail marked by William Kamkwamba.

The Greening of Africa

All over Africa, individual entrepreneurs and local businesses are making small but significant steps in a positive direction. Kissima Basse, for example, is an entrepreneur based in Mopti, Mali, who is enjoying considerable success importing energy-efficient vapor air coolers (*brumisateurs*) from France. Future project plans include cultivating organic fair-trade cotton and using it for garment production locally. This strategy will provide the locals with environmentally superior goods and obviate the current high-transport production model, in which the cheap raw material is exported and the more expensive readymade garments are later imported, at a cost that is much higher both to the customer and the environment. "The people that own industries in Mali don't care about the environment," he laments. "I want to use my influence to change this, and make Mali green." Coming from a family of entrepreneurs which always has had a focus on the social benefits that a business should generate, Kissima is also running a program that provides schooling to street children and is in the planning stage of building a rural hospital (paid for out of the profits of his business). "It's thanks to my mother," he explains. "At my mother's small textile dye business in Bamako she's always provided literacy training for her female employees. She taught me how important it is to share wealth with those who have less, and to do my little bit to make life better for my fellow countrymen and -women." Those African entrepreneurs who share this thinking rarely do it for marketing purposes, nor to claim corporate social responsibility, but simply because doing good is good.

As the financial crisis in Europe and North America has led to a massive homecoming of emigrants, many are bringing with them bright ideas regarding innovation and sustainable entrepreneurship. The entrepreneurs Tunji Abdul and Kabir Audu returned to Nigeria after 10 years abroad, bursting with ideas on how to improve living standards and run more environmentally conscious businesses in their home country. Their start-up, the real estate group HCI, is now developing the first "sustainable" high-rise in Nigeria, a mixed-use waterfront development in the country's economic center, Lagos. These buildings will follow the principles of resource and energy efficiency, low-energy materials, ecologically and socially sensitive land use, and reduced greenhouse emissions.

A lot of eco-innovation entrepreneurship is also born out of aid-and-development agencies and organizations and mainly deals with implementing eco-efficient technologies already developed elsewhere. An example is the World Bank–led project "Lighting Africa," which in collaboration with local and international industries supports the private sector to "develop, accelerate, and sustain the market for modern off-grid lighting technologies tailored to the needs of African consumers." Lighting Africa's main innovation is applying energy-efficient light-emitting diode (LED) lights along with related technologies such as solar street lights, aiming to help electrify rural areas and replace costly and polluting kerosene while making electric light available for more people. These projects are also executed in cooperation with civil society and NGOs. Cycling Out of Poverty, for instance, is a Dutch NGO that provides microcredit loans in a number of African countries for establishing bicycle-centered businesses. Along with the funding they also offer training in bicycle maintenance and repair and help in adapting traditional bicycles for commercial purposes. Among the successful businesses that have been born out of this project is a private ambulance service in Uganda, and tricycles for transport of small school children in Ghana.

Certain governments around Africa are also seeking innovation as they pursue development. Rwanda is a good example: Only 15 years ago, the country was ravaged by civil war and genocide, but today is emerging as a regional hub for information and communications technologies and is focusing the rebuilding of its economy on becoming a knowledge-based economy as it works simultaneously toward its development goals. "If we have to wait for everybody, for every household in Rwanda to have good drinking water and sufficient food and shelter," says Albert Butare, the Rwandan minister for energy and communications, "we shall wait forever."

Some examples of technological innovation are really transformational. A well-known example is that of the extremely innovative Kenyan mobile banking system M-Pesa, which is a technological frog-leap so impressive that it over-shadows most mobile banking efforts in the developed world. Nine million of the total Kenyan population of 16 million subscribe to the service, which allows people to pay bills with their mobile phones and use ATMs without having an ATM card or even a bank account. This system obviates the physical infrastructure of traditional banks; the energy needed to build, light, and cool the buildings and to run the banking hardware would far outweigh the environmental costs of the virtual banking network. Local entrepreneurs are even using this technology for rural development when, for instance, companies install water wells in rural villages at no initial cost and are later paid on an as-you-go basis through mobile banking.

Problems of Population and Peak Oil

If necessity is the mother of invention, then Africa is ripe for groundbreaking, mind-boggling inventions. Environmental issues include desertification, loss of biodiversity, deforestation, and loss of agricultural productivity due to climate change, along with increasing waste-related challenges. Social problems are also plentiful if the Millennium Development Goals [established by the United Nations] are taken as an index of the need. The approaching demographic explosion in Africa is expected to worsen those challenges: The current African population of around 1 billion is expected to reach around 1.7 billion by the year 2050. Growing populations have already hampered many countries in sub-Saharan Africa in improving child mortality and other wellbeing indices.

The coming decades will also see decreasing oil reserves globally, meaning that petroleum-based activities will become more expensive. According to data from the Organization of Petroleum Exporting Countries (OPEC), the average price for petroleum in 2000 was US$27.60 per barrel; 10 years later it had risen to $75.49. (In between the price fluctuated wildly, peaking at over $130 per barrel in the summer of 2008). This peak was indirectly one of the causes of the hike in the price of staple foods around the world that helped provoke riots and political instability in various African countries. The jury is still out on when exactly peak oil will happen, but one study for the U.S. Army warned that in a worst-case scenario there could be a massive oil shortage, 10 million barrels per day, by 2015.

Shortages of this severity will lead to huge differences in development possibilities, in the traditional understanding of the term, between countries with stronger or weaker economies. Rising oil prices will affect African economies in two main ways. First, they will mean that using petrol or diesel for running machinery and vehicles will become more costly and therefore less viable for cash-poor economies, and could further force governments to spend increasing parts of their budgets on fuel, rather than urgent development needs such as schools and health care. Second, global transport will also become more expensive, meaning that importing goods from faraway countries will in most cases make them significantly more expensive and put them out of reach of many Africans.

Peak oil and development challenges are therefore extremely important to take into consideration for entrepreneurs, since it is the sort of evolution that will determine whether their businesses are winners or losers in the marketplace. Innovation will have to focus on locally available raw materials to the greatest extent possible and involve as little transport as possible. Africa's low dependency on oil—the seven relatively populous countries of Democratic Republic of Congo, Ethiopia, Ghana, Kenya, Sudan, Tanzania, and Uganda have about the same population as the United States but consume less than one-sixtieth the oil—could thus be a blessing in disguise, although this comparative advantage could easily be lost if development and innovation patterns focus on "catching-up" strategies that emulate Western development.

Investing in Durable Products

One strategy for leapfrogging in a direction that decouples development and economic growth from environmental damage is what inventor Saul Griffith calls "heirloom design." Griffith describes an heirloom design as "something that will not only last through your lifetime and into the next generation, but that you also desire to keep that long, because it's beautiful, functional, and timeless"—products that have lives beyond fads and fashion and that respond to true human needs, not just desires.

A key feature of heirloom designs is that they are designed to be fixed, not thrown out, which in turn demands a lot more skilled labor during their lifetimes for maintenance, repairs, and upgrades. Again, Africa is in a position to show the developed world the way to go. When designing such products, entrepreneurs would have to take into consideration that repair manuals must be provided, electronic components should be replaced with mechanical ones when possible (less toxic, easier to repair), and spare parts must be easily available for decades, according to Griffith.

In Africa, where labor is abundant and cash less so, it makes even more sense to invent durable products that can be repaired and upgraded, rather than cheap goods that are discarded after use. Economic constraints mean that most consumer goods are already being used much more efficiently in developing countries through reuse and repairs. In developed countries labor is so costly that it is often cheaper to buy a new product than to repair an old one. (So limited have practical fixing skills become here in the West that many socio-environmental movements in developed countries, such as Transition Towns, have "re-skilling" as a main pillar.)

Heirloom design products can thus generate significant employment beyond the production phase. "In developing countries, all innovation must, by default, focus on generating employment," says Dr. Sherwat Elwan, an expert in innovation and technology management at the German University in Cairo, Egypt. . . .

Social Cohesion as a Business Strategy

A final potential advantage for African eco-innovation is the continued existence of non-competitive societies and economies, where the greater communal good is still in many aspects more important than the individual accumulation of profits. One example of this is the West African gift economy, or *dama*. In these countries, this parallel economy has thrived for centuries in spite of the rapid commercialization of life there. At the center of the gift economy is the concept of "I give, therefore I am someone important," and the complementing notion that "I receive, therefore I let you be someone important." If you receive, you are also indirectly required to share with someone else when you are able. Further down the line, the original giver might be the one benefitting from the gift-giving again—or maybe not. We saw how the entrepreneur Kissima Basse shares his profits with the community; another example is seen when women in Mali give birth. Friends and family provide the mother and the baby with all they need for the first 40 days, so that they can rest and gather strength before facing hard work again. Those with extra food share that; those with extra money share that. Those with neither provide services such as babysitting or cleaning. In this symbiosis the giver and the receiver have equal importance in keeping society together, and making sure that everybody's needs are met.

These customs are based on the understanding that a wealthy community is one where people are interconnected and look after each other. At the other end of the spectrum are individualist cultures where competition replaces collaboration and winner-take-all sentiments rule. Perhaps not surprisingly, highly individualist cultures such as those in the

United States and Western Europe also have larger ecological impacts. As countries develop economically, their populations often go through a cultural transformation and morph into western-style individualist consumers. It therefore seems that if a culture manages to stay true to its collectivist roots and maintain the focus on communal wellbeing, it can also keep unsustainable individualist consumption patterns, and the related ecological impacts, at arm's length.

As an added benefit, the cohesion of such cultures creates increased social stability, which again spills over to a better environment—in terms of ecology, business, and even governance. The challenge lies in finding ways that entrepreneurship and innovation can nourish such collective wellbeing, while simultaneously taking into consideration the planetary limits. This is largely unexplored territory.

Entrepreneurship for a Sustainable Africa

Decoupling innovation from traditional production and consumption patterns may appear unrealistic, but it is a highly necessary move on a planet with finite resources. An important step is to get a better understanding of the difference between wants and needs. If "wants" are to dictate innovation, then it becomes difficult to use planetary resource limitations as guidelines, since wants are unlimited.

Entrepreneurship in twenty-first-century Africa must also be about creating sustainable alternatives that suit the kind of development and societies Africans want. "Poor people in Kenya—and by extension much of Africa—know exactly why they are poor, and what they need to do to escape poverty," says Fuchaka Waswa, a senior lecturer in environmental studies at Kenyatta University in Nairobi, Kenya. "If you have a spine [thorn] in your shoe, you are the only one who knows about it and its real impact. It is you who must take action and free yourself from discomfort. As such, foreign NGOs and development agencies fit better as facilitators for these bottom-up strategies, rather than designers of solutions."

This has tremendous impacts on the kind of innovation that the continent should seek. While it is not for any outsider to prescribe a development path for Africa, it seems that the continent would do well in the twenty-first century if it strove to avoid the quagmire of the development history traced by the global North to date: resource-intensive, wasteful, self-delusional about planetary limits, and heedless of the damage done to the biosphere. If Africa is to make a place for itself in a resource-constrained world, it should focus on strategies that play to its strengths: creativity, social cohesion, experience with leapfrogging destructive phases of development, and keen comprehension of local needs and wants. The continent might even find itself better off, down the road, than its "richer" neighbors, who still seem to believe that "business as usual" can continue indefinitely. To the contrary, as Tellus Institute founder Paul Raskin has put it, "It is business as usual that is the Utopian fantasy; forging a new vision is the pragmatic necessity."

Periodical Bibliography

The following articles have been selected to supplement the diverse views presented in this chapter.

Tony Binns	"Making Development Work in Africa (part 2): Enhancing Sustainability," *Geography*, Summer 2009.
Richard J. Blaustein	"The Green Revolution Arrives in Africa," *Bioscience*, January 2008.
Deborah Fahy Bryceson	"Sub-Saharan Africa's Vanishing Peasantries and the Specter of a Global Food Crisis," *Monthly Review: An Independent Socialist Magazine*, July/August 2009.
Robert Feldman	"The Root Causes of Terrorism: Why Parts of Africa Might Never Be at Peace," *Defense & Security Analysis*, December 2009.
Mo Ibrahim	"Africa Ready for Take-Off!," *New African*, November 2010.
Ethan B. Kapstein	"Africa's Capitalist Revolution," *Foreign Affairs*, July/August 2009.
Claire Keton	"Bridging the Gap in South Africa," *Bulletin of the World Health Organization*, November 2010.
Raj Patel, Eric Holt-Gimenez, and Annie Shattuck	"Ending Africa's Hunger," *Nation*, September 21, 2009.
Karen Rothmyer	"Brace Yourself: Good News on Africa," *Nation*, June 21, 2010.
Dan Taylor	"Africa Doesn't Need a Green Revolution: It Needs Agroecology," *Ecologist*, October 2009.

OPPOSING
VIEWPOINTS®
SERIES

CHAPTER 2

Does Africa Need Foreign Aid?

Chapter Preface

In her 2009 book *Dead Aid: Why Aid Is Not Working and How There Is a Better Way for Africa*, pro-market economist Dambisa Moyo makes the controversial argument that foreign aid harms Africa by fostering a culture of dependency on Western handouts and abetting corruption in African governments that ultimately discourage any fiscal policy changes. Drawing on her own experiences growing up in Zambia, Moyo attests, "The notion that aid can alleviate systemic poverty, and has done so, is a myth. Millions in Africa today are poorer because of aid." Although Moyo is not the first observer to criticize the philosophy of foreign aid, her book stirred global debate about what she termed "the pop culture of aid"—a phenomenon promoted by celebrities and government officials that focuses on Western nations' inability to give enough rather than on the changes within African governments that would facilitate economic growth. A supporter of Moyo's argument, Paul Kagame, the president of Rwanda, told Britain's *Financial Times* on May 7, 2009, "We appreciate support from the outside, but it should be support for what we intend to achieve ourselves. No one should pretend that they care about our nations more than we do; or assume that they know what is good for us better than we do ourselves. They should, in fact, respect us for wanting to decide our own fate."

Some analysts, though, fear that letting Africa decide its own fate may be too rosy a stance given the poor governance in many developing African counties. In his January 30, 2009, review of *Dead Aid* in *The Independent* (a United Kingdom newspaper), Paul Collier, an economics professor who taught Moyo at Harvard and Oxford Universities, claims, "I doubt that many of Africa's problems can be attributed to aid." He still believes that aid can be used as a tool to bring about needed changes but suggests that some improvements are in order. "My preferred alternative is to strengthen its potential for 'governance conditionality': aid agencies should insist on both transparent budgeting and free and fair elections," Collier writes. Kevin Watkins, a senior visiting research fellow with the Global Economic Governance Programme (GEG) at Oxford University endorses this view. Criticizing Moyo in an April 24, 2009, opinion piece for the *Huffington Post*, Watkins insists that foreign donors know that aid is not the cure for Africa's problems but can be a powerful influential force in making corrupt regimes more accountable to their people. Even when such enticements fail, Watkins maintains, aid has directly improved health care and education for many Africans, and such victories cannot be ignored in discussing the possible termination of foreign aid.

The viewpoints presented in the following chapter further these debates. The authors weigh the benefits and drawbacks of foreign aid, and they discuss the changes needed in donor and recipient nations to make aid more effective in reducing poverty and stimulating economic enterprise in Africa.

> *"Today's foreign aid now looks for ways to stimulate private-sector solutions that will be sustainable over the long term ... and the programs that work with host governments are designed to require local governments to take on aid responsibility."*

Foreign Aid Benefits Africa

Scott Baldauf

In the following viewpoint, Scott Baldauf disputes critics who charge that aid to Africa is doing more harm than good. According to Baldauf, effectively targeted aid (whether medical, financial, or technological) has benefited many impoverished nations and should not be slashed because of US budget cuts. Scott Baldauf is a staff writer for the Christian Science Monitor, *a US-based international newspaper.*

As you read, consider the following questions:

1. What is a critique of foreign aid, as given by American voters, as reported by Baldauf?

2. What percentage of the federal budget is spent on foreign aid, according to the author?

3. How does Baldauf respond to the claim that Africa is poorer today because of aid?

When it comes to structural adjustment, the US government generally plays the role of the donor nation, setting conditions on debtor nations in order to get their fiscal houses in order.

This year [2011], the US government, having reached its self-imposed limit for how much money it can borrow, is scrambling to pay its bills and keep its creditors at bay.

With President [Barack] Obama's administration and the Republican-controlled Congress debating how to cut back government spending, everything is on the table, including America's $50 billion overseas programs, including foreign aid.

Implications for Foreign Aid

But a number of high-level US State Department and aid officials, on a recent visit to South Africa, said that foreign aid programs such as former President George Bush's ongoing President's Emergency Program for AIDS Relief (PEPFAR) enjoy bipartisan support. And the US government is both changing the way it gives out foreign aid, empowering local governments to take on their own development, and remaining engaged with a developing world that increasingly has choices of whom it does business with.

"The logo of USAID says, 'from the American people,' but I think the American people increasingly understand that our development commitments in Africa also generate outcomes for the American people," says Raj Shah, the chief administrator for the US Agency for International Development (USAID), which handles most of the US government's foreign development assistance.

Foreign Aid Is Important

"It's an expression of our moral values when we are able to save lives on this continent and protect young children from starving or protect people with HIV from dying when they don't need to die," Mr. Shah says. "But we also know these outcomes keep us safe and lay the groundwork for economic stability and growth."

Foreign aid to Africa may have bipartisan support in Congress, but ordinary American voters often see foreign aid as a colossal waste of taxpayer money—while also vastly overestimating the US government's foreign aid budget. In a November 2010 poll conducted by WorldPublicOpinion.org and Knowledge Networks, Americans were asked what percentage of the US federal budget was spent on foreign aid; the median answer was 25 percent. When asked what would be the "appropriate" percentage of the budget spent on foreign aid; the median answer was a much more parsimonious 10 percent figure. The US actually spends only 1 percent of its federal budget on foreign aid.

Worthwhile Aid That Makes a Difference

If budget cutters were to go after giant projects, then the six-year-old initiative PEPFAR would present an attractive project. At $7.2 billion in the Fiscal 2012 budget, it is the largest single foreign aid program of its kind, not only in the US federal budget, but also in the world. In South Africa alone, 917,000 men, women, and children are able to receive Anti-Retro Viral (ARV) treatment each year because of the PEPFAR program, and doctors estimate that some 114,000 babies worldwide have been born HIV-free because of ARV treatments made available to their HIV-positive parents.

Yet like a Wal-Mart that keeps costs low by buying in bulk, PEPFAR's very size may actually give it an advantage in bringing down the costs of its programs. In the past year, PEPFAR has negotiated with drug companies to reduce the cost of

ARVs by 50 percent, thereby allowing it to increase its global reach to 3.2 million HIV patients. In addition, because PEP-FAR was designed to help recipient countries manage their own HIV crisis response efforts, PEPFAR is doing what few aid projects do. It is putting itself, slowly, steadily, out of business. Here in South Africa, for instance, all purchase of ARVs is done with South African tax money, but purchased through the PEPFAR's bulk-buying system.

This makes PEPFAR a possible model for other US aid programs, USAID Deputy Secretary of State Thomas Nides said in a recent meeting with reporters in Johannesburg.

"As someone who has now probably in the last 72 hours gone to four or five sites where these dollars are spent . . . they're fantastic dollars spent," said Mr. Nides. But "this program was always set up to transition this program to allow the country to take on more and more of the responsibility of the program, not only for it to execute the program, to manage the clinics distribution centers, but to take on more of what we believe is their responsibility. We're well aware this cannot happen overnight but I think if you talk to the South Africans, as I have, they're very much desirous to do this."

Changes to Foreign Aid

Some economists see the current budget crisis as an opportunity to change entirely the way in which US foreign aid is spent, while others like former World Bank economist and Zambian native Dambisa Moyo favor discarding all foreign aid altogether.

"Millions in Africa are poorer today because of aid; misery and poverty have not ended but have increased," Ms. Moyo wrote in her provocative 2009 book "Dead Aid." Because foreign aid generally ends up being administered by incompetent or corrupt local government officials, it often ends up enriching the few while destroying economic opportunities for the poorer majority, Moyo argues. "Aid has been, and continues to be, an unmitigated political, economic, and humanitarian disaster for most parts of the developing world."

Yet such critiques of foreign aid are misapplied, says Shah, the USAID administrator. Today's foreign aid now looks for ways to stimulate private-sector solutions that will be sustainable over the long term, he says, and the programs that work with host governments are designed to require local governments to take on aid responsibility.

"South Korea had a lower food production per capita, a higher degree of malnutrition and hunger, and a lower economic growth rate than Kenya in the early 1960s, and USAID partnered with South Korea over a number of decades and today South Korea is a donor country," says Shah. "President Obama believes that African leaders and entrepreneurs who make the right decisions can achieve that kind of success and has asked us to make sure we're good partners in that process."

As for the budget, it's not over yet, Shah says. The budget "is a real fight for us. But I would point out that members of both parties have fought for our development commitments to Africa."

"*Despite the massive injection of aid over the past five decades, Africa, rather than achieve economic growth and development, has become more dependent, with standards of living experiencing a net decline.*"

Foreign Aid Does Not Benefit Africa

Mathew K. Jallow

In the following viewpoint, Mathew K. Jallow contends that foreign aid is doing more harm than good in Africa. According to Jallow, aid is disbursed broadly to African governments that siphon off the funds for private use. However, corruption is only one of the downsides of foreign aid, in Jallow's view. He also claims that misdirected aid has competed with and, in some cases, ruined domestic markets and that foreign governments often use aid as a tool to create dependency among recipient nations. Jallow insists that aid should not be permitted to stifle African productivity or else many developing nations on the continent will remain caught in the trap of poverty and poor governance. Jallow is a Gambian journalist and human rights activist living in exile in the United States.

As you read, consider the following questions:

1. As Jallow reports, why does the United Nations Development Program describe the 1980s as "the lost decade" in terms of foreign aid transfers?

2. According to the author, what happened to Somalia's agricultural market between 1979 and 1984? And what does he believe caused this change?

3. Under what circumstances does foreign aid serve a useful purpose, in Jallow's opinion?

The African continent has struggled with chronic poverty and under-development since the advent of political independence more than fifty years ago, and many Africans view this problem as one of Africa's own making. African development experts and academics have blamed foreign aid for the continued and seemingly intractable development crisis confronting the continent. Africa's war on poverty is perceived as amounting to begging and submissiveness, leading to reforms that have made Africans poorer. The contention among many African experts is that the more the developed north cooperated with the south, the poorer Africa became. And increasingly, even tangible western generosity has failed to impress many Africans. Foreign aid has generally benefited the ruling elites in Africa, by among other things, enabling and perpetuating corrupt governments' hold on power, and by extension, entrenching the pervasive underdevelopment. Over the past five decades, foreign emergency assistance to Africa has helped to avert hardship for many of Africa's poor, but failed to promote any significant economic development. Foreign aid is provided with the conviction that real economic development begins when the emphasis is placed on providing aid to poor rural and urban communities.

Breeding Dependency

Providing assistance to Africa's poor is a noble cause, but the five-decades-long campaign of aid has turned out to be what one critic called "a theater of the absurd." To-date, the record of western aid to Africa has been significant, amounting to more than $500 billion between 1960 and 1997, which is the equivalent of four Marshall Plans [the Marshall Plan rebuilt Europe after World War II] being pumped into Sub-Saharan Africa. And today, the national budgets of most Sub-Saharan African countries are dependent on foreign aid for up to eighty percent of their annual budgets. Apart from the relief aid and economic development, foreign aid assistance was also provided to support reforms and policy adjustment programs. And between 1981 and 1991 alone, The World Bank provided $20 billion towards Africa's structural adjustment programs. The purpose of the programs was to make public institutions, government agencies, and bureaucracies in Africa more transparent, effective, efficient and accountable. It is baffling that Africa still suffers from a poverty trap, considering the depth of governments' corruption and the missing billions in export earnings from oil, gas, diamonds and other resources. The idea of foreign aid was compatible with the central theme of economic development, and was accepted as a possible escape from the chronic underdevelopment that is characterized by undeveloped infrastructure and dualistic economies. The persistence of the deplorable economic conditions in Africa has become the primary reason for the relentless search for realistic and durable solutions to the continent's development woes, even as the need for aid is intermittently reinforced by the fact that Africa's underdevelopment is accentuated by periodic global economic recession.

When it was conceived after World War II, U.S. foreign aid was designed to serve two conceptually interdependent, but potentially conflicting sets of goals: first, the diplomatic and strategic goals that advance U.S. short-term political and long-term strategic interests; and secondly, the development and humanitarian goals that sought a long-term economic growth, political stability, and the short-term alleviation of suffering. The U.S. Foreign Assistance Act of 1973 stressed the need to promote equity, minimum standards of living and per capita growth. Since then, the U.S. foreign assistance statutes have gone through several changes; each with its own objective and, some would argue, defined by global politics rather than by any humane consideration. The concept of "Basic Human Needs," under the U.S. Foreign Assistance statutes, can be seen as paradoxical if one considers the foreign assistance legislation as the expression of the primary function of foreign aid. The position of the U.S. as observed by development experts is that developmental and humanitarian programs received substantial funding only when they coincided with U.S. diplomatic and strategic interests. And despite the massive injection of aid over the past five decades, Africa, rather than achieve economic growth and development, has become more dependent, with standards of living experiencing a net decline. Studies show that there is overwhelming evidence that foreign aid has helped to under-write the misguided policies of the corrupt and bloated government bureaucracies across Africa. [An] Oxford International Group study revealed that the external stock of capital held by Africans in overseas accounts, was between $700 billion and $800 billion in 2005, and nearly 40% of Africa's aggregate wealth was stacked in foreign bank accounts in Europe, United States and Japan. Africa's foreign assistance is significant when we look at the overall economic situation, and African governments have become dependent on aid for the survival of their people and governments.

Aid Is Slowing Growth

The concept of aid is relatively new, and it's basically the transfer of resources from the rich countries to poor ones for the purpose of development. Foreign aid is primarily the official government-to-government transfer of financial and technical resources for the programs of social and economic development. The main objective of aid is to produce accelerated economic growth, combined with higher standards of consumption, but as we have seen, aid is very much influenced by prevailing regional or global political climates. Due to political necessities, donors often exert pressure for political and policy reasons, thereby making dependence on aid shaky and unreliable. Additionally, those charged with making decisions on aid allocation, generally do not have a good grasp of issues facing developing and poor countries; consequently, the rationale behind most aid disbursement decisions are usually fraught with poor judgments and inconsistencies. The disadvantages of aid include the fact that funding provided is usually tied to the fact it must be spent in the donor countries regardless of the high cost of goods and services. Rather than create wealth, prosperity and economic development, most Africans have over the past few decades realized a net decline in their standards of living. Research shows that over the period that foreign aid was being pumped into Africa, the per capita GDP [gross domestic product] declined by an average of 0.59 percent annually, between 1975 and 2000. The Heritage Foundation in 1985 concluded that foreign aid is not the answer to Africa's economic troubles; and in fact, the organization maintained that aid was contributing to Africa's underdevelopment woes. It is now a popular belief that foreign aid has been found to do more harm, leading to the situation where Africans have failed to set their own pace and direction of development free of external interference. The United Nations Conference on Trade and Development admits that aid to Africa has not been successful and despite many years of policy reform, no Sub-Saharan country has completed its adjustment program or achieved any sustained economic growth. Similarly, a Heritage Foundation study found that foreign aid retards the process of economic growth and the accumulation

Aid Creates Government Gangsters

Aid kills democracy. It makes being in power enormously lucrative. When going into (corrupt) politics or becoming a (corrupt) state official is a more attractive career option than starting a business, it will obviously end in tears. It means that politics attracts gangsters, indeed creates gangsters. The gangsters don't want to relinquish power, so another set of gangsters, thinly dressed as liberators, arm themselves and make war.

Martin Durkin, interviewed by Jamie Glazov,
FrontPage Magazine, *December 3, 2008.*

of wealth. The Foundation argued aid dependency pulls entrepreneurship and intellectual capital into non-productive activities, thereby blunting the entrepreneurial spirits of many Africans.

Africa on the Decline

The decades of financial and technical aid transfers to Africa have not fostered economic growth, rather, it has left seventy countries, primarily in Sub-Saharan Africa, poorer than they were in 1980, and 43 are worse off than they were in 1970. The United Nations Development Program [UNDP] describes the 1980's, the period of highest foreign aid transfer to Africa, as the "lost decade." Over much of that decade, 100 countries, mostly in Africa, suffered major economic decline or net stagnation, and the conclusion is that foreign aid failed to create economic growth in aid recipient countries. The old belief that aid transfer allowed poor countries to escape the poverty trap has been refuted, because research has proved that poverty, contrary to the popular belief, is not caused by capital shortage. In fact, studies show that there is no correlation between aid and economic development, rather, most aid recipient countries have become and remained more dependent on foreign aid. Additionally, a World Bank study showed that food aid budgets in developed nations were mainly guided by prospects for commercial exports of surplus from donor countries, and not determined in accordance with the needs and objectives of recipient countries to reduce dependence on imported food. Donors reduce food aid budgets when the prospect for commercial exports are good, and increase them when the prospects are poor. A U.S. 1997 General Accounting Office report, criticized USAID [US Agency for International Development] for having no strategies for the assessment of the impact of its programs in enhancing the food security, and further, the Agency could not determine whether food aid was an efficient means of accomplishing food security goals in aid recipient African countries. Poor policy choices in Africa have caused development there to first stagnate and decline over the past several decades. In 1960, South Korea was as poor as the African countries, but thirty years later, the country was wealthy enough to offer aid to Africa. Altogether, South East Asian countries have achieved phenomenal development in the past five decades, and many have joined the industrialized countries of the world. Critics now contend that foreign aid to Africa must be changed for a number of reasons, but mainly because it has not worked. Further, they argue that most aid initiatives are well thought out, and most of the funding intended for projects rarely reaches the intended target groups. A study found that in Uganda, less than 30 per cent of the aid earmarked for primary education actually reached the intended schools. The missing funds were stolen, wasted or re-apportioned to priorities identified by politicians or middle level and senior government officials. To address the persistent failure of Sub-Saharan Africa, donors have identified capacity building as the answer to the perennial problem of underdevelopment in Africa. Since 1980, about 4 billion dollars has been spent each year in training, technical assistance and institutional strengthening capacities in Africa.

Failed Aid Experiments

More than six decades of foreign aid has not changed Africa's latent capacity; moreover, professionals from around the continent are leaving for other countries in the west at an alarming rate. Today, many aid agencies are acknowledging that there is greater pressure to commit money grandly than to spend it wisely in Africa. In 1976, Tanzania began the $220 million Mufundi paper mill factory project financed by the World Bank. The project turned out to be a total failure, yet for twenty years, Tanzanians paid the bill for that ill-thought-out experiment. In the early 1990's, the UNDP spent $900,000 over a three year period trying unsuccessfully to show farmers in north-east Ivory Coast how to cultivate onions. Meanwhile, 90 miles north, in neighboring Burkina Faso, the farmers there were growing onions profitably under similar agricultural conditions, but without any foreign aid. A World Bank finding on food import into Somalia in 1998 concluded that aid had methodically undermined Somalia's civil society. Somalia had become more dependent on imported food than any other country in Sub-Saharan Africa. The report noted that until food aid began to arrive in Somalia, the economy was predominantly an agricultural and pastoral economy. And up until the early seventies, Somalia was self-sufficient in food grains production; however, Somalia's share of food imported in total volume of food consumption rose from less than 33 per cent in 1979 to over 63 per cent in 1984. This sea change ironically coincided with the period of highest food aid distribution to that country. By increasing the supply of food aid, Somalia's domestic food prices were dampened, and the prices of local food crops were prevented from rising, thus reducing the incentives for domestic food crop producers. This exacerbated Somalia's food deficit. Mismanagement and corruption in the administration of food aid distribution in Africa is pervasive in the absence of efficient and accountable institutions to oversee and institute fair and just aid distribution practices. But, critics of aid say donors are also complicit in the failure of aid distribution in Africa, as there are no effective monitoring mechanisms, and this gives the politicians and bureaucrats the opportunity to rob what is intended for the people. A former U.S Ambassador to Ghana, Edward P. Bryan, admitted that foreign donors have allowed what he describes as "a small, clever class that inherited power from the colonial masters to take us to the cleaners." It will take a lot of resources and time to turn Africa around. In March 1990, a Paris daily, *Le Monde*, wrote, "Every franc given to impoverished Africans, comes back to France or is smuggled into Switzerland by African bureaucrats and politicians." And critics contend that donor agencies knew or should have known the motivation and activities of corrupt African leaders who spirit away billions into Swiss Banks and other western bank accounts. Even famine relief aid is not spared. As early as the late 1980's, a former head of [Doctors Without Borders], Dr. Rory Branman, lamented the failure of aid to Africa, saying, "We have been duped." "The Western governments and humanitarian groups," he said, have "unwittingly fueled and are continuing to fuel an operation that will be described in hindsight in a few years' time as one of the greatest slaughters of our time." The World Bank admitted that in most cases Western donors knew that up to 30 per cent of the loans to African countries and governments went directly into the bank accounts of corrupt officials, yet the Bank considered these officials and their governments as partners in development.

Ulterior Motives in Gift Giving

But, foreign aid is full of ambiguities and double bottoms. It does not fit neatly into any one of the three ways people are said to go about their material transaction; i.e; coercion, exchange and gift giving. Because it is tied with geo-politics, trade and banking, foreign aid cannot be classified purely as gift-giving. During its first four decades, victory in the Cold War was the compelling and pre-eminent drive in the regime of aid giving. Today, experts have identified the predominant motives for aid giving as strategic socio-political, mercantile, and humanitarian and ethical. Official aid is seldom the tool of altruism alone, because the direction of foreign aid is dictated by political and strategic considerations, much more than the economic needs and policy performance of the recipient. However, the motives behind aid never come in fixed and stable proportions. Perhaps the one safest generalization to make is that foreign aid, when used alone or in combination with other policy instruments, has a unique ability to allow the donors to demonstrate compassion, while simultaneously pursuing a variety of other ulterior motives and objectives. In the U.S., the realization that aid has failed to provide economic growth and development over several decades, prompted the U.S. Government to try different ways of administering its foreign aid. Officials in the [Ronald] Reagan administration promoted direct local participation in the planning, implementation and overall control of projects. And USAID further made efforts to recruit in-country field staffs that are experienced in and sensitive to Africa's development processes and institutions. U.S. government officials recommended that Congress monitor the activities of USAID, but without getting involved in any of the operational decision-making. Yet, this did not address the goal conflict that has created the paradox of foreign aid. Countries receiving foreign aid in amounts that are sufficient to stimulate development along the lines of the Basic Human Needs mandate, are precisely the countries that are important to the diplomatic and strategic goals of the United States. A Cato Institute study found little evidence that better targeting and management enabled foreign aid to achieve self-sustaining growth in poor African countries. Additionally, the U.S. Congressional Budget

Office warned that aid can inhibit the commitment to reforms of even the more responsible African governments, and without reform, aid can reinforce policies that do not further development. The failure of Africa's development assistance has allowed poor countries to delay reform, thereby worsening the underlying problems. Empirical evidence suggests that the greater a country's dependence on aid, the worst the quality of its public institutions. Poverty is a justification for aid, but it is seldom the main criterion used for allocating it.

Aid Is Not a Substitute for Productivity

The public image of foreign aid is of Western beneficence; nevertheless, studies show in some cases, foreign worker remittance to their countries of origin far exceeds the annual aid transfers from some European countries. In 1998, the officially recorded remittance from the Netherlands to forty-two low-income developing countries exceeded U.S.$1 billion; a sum equivalent to 115 percent of Dutch aid to those countries. In the non-oil-producing countries in Africa, trade losses between 1970 and 1997 represented almost minus 120% of GDP. Ironically, the World Bank estimated that the purchasing power in those African countries would be considerably lower in 2010 than they were back in 1997. Foreign aid serves a useful purpose when it is provided to alleviate temporary hardship as in cases of natural disasters such as droughts, but, experience in Africa has proved that aid recipients could easily construe foreign aid as a substitution to their own productivity. Across the continent, food aid has suppressed food production, undermining the prices of locally produced foods. Agricultural production has declined significantly, as farmers migrate to urban centers to create a shortage of farm workers and exacerbate food production deficits. As mentioned earlier, a major debilitating by-product of foreign aid to Africa is the culture of corruption that has taken root at every level of every government. Today, corruption has become the way of life in every country in Sub-Saharan Africa, and the theft, bribery and embezzlement of aid and other government resources are so endemic, they are not considered as crimes. African politicians and government officials have engaged in corruption practices, and a 2004–2005 World Bank Report showed that $148 billion were embezzled out of Africa by politicians and bureaucrats; a significant amount of it being aid and loans earmarked for development activities to benefit Africa's poor. Without transparency, accountability, and good governance, Africa's future will continue to remain bleak.

> "Foreign aid has generally engendered a welfare mentality. This means that the continent continues to lack the technology to exploit its enormous wealth of resources or to influence the relative intensity with which its different factors of production can be used."

Africa Needs Trade, Not Only Foreign Aid

Richard Ilorah

In the following viewpoint, Richard Ilorah claims that foreign aid has stifled productivity in Africa (especially sub-Saharan Africa) and has bred a culture of dependency. Ilorah asserts that better trade relationships would improve this problematic situation, but Africa's trade patterns have so far been unhelpful to building stronger economies. Ilorah blames this on international policies that punish Africa for trying to export finished products (such as manufactured goods) instead of primary commodities (such as food and oil). He believes African nations must create trading collectives to increase their bargaining strength and throw off some of the restrictive policies that are holding African

Richard Ilorah, "Trade, Aid and National Development in Africa," *Development Southern Africa*, vol. 25, no. 1, March 2008. Copyright © 2010. All rights reserved. Reproduced by permission.

nations hostage to the whims of Western trade organizations. Only then will African economies begin to diversify and attract investment as well as compete in global markets, Ilorah maintains. Ilorah is a professor of economics at the University of Limpopo in South Africa.

As you read, consider the following questions:

1. According to Ilorah, in what nations and regions do foreign investors typically invest?

2. As Ilorah reports, how much do US cotton subsidies cost West African economies each year?

3. What percentage of the world's mineral reserves are held in African nations, according to the author?

Trade promotes competition, investments, knowledge transfer and growth. Poor trade in Africa compromises growth through low productivity, often culminating in dependence on foreign aid and heavy indebtedness. In 2005, Africa's total external debt stood at $318.5 billion, corresponding to 35.7 per cent of its gross domestic product (GDP). The continent's excess debt often results in debt repayment burdens, for which poor trade performance and policies are to blame. The World Bank noted that the continent's performance is often matched by the trend in the official development assistance (ODA) from wealthy countries rather than by the world economic outlook and that ODA flows are equivalent to a sizeable share of the GDP and domestic investment in many African countries. For example, the ODA as a percentage of GDP for the entire continent during 1975–84, 1985–9 and the 1990s was 3.6 per cent, 5 per cent and 4.9 per cent, respectively and for the sub-Saharan countries 4.2 per cent, 7.9 per cent and 6.3 per cent. During the same periods, the net ODA as a percentage of gross domestic investment for the continent as a whole was 14.2 per cent, 24.3 per cent and 23.9 per cent and for the sub-Saharan countries 21.8 per cent, 49.4 per cent and 36.4 per cent, respectively.

African countries have continuously expected to use foreign aid to fill the gap between the domestically available supplies of savings and the level of these resources necessary to achieve investment targets and growth or to fill the gap between targeted foreign exchange requirements and the revenue derived from net export earnings plus foreign private investment. Since the majority of these countries have barely any savings, in view of their very small earnings from exports of just a handful of primary commodities and the lack of foreign private investment in the region, these gaps are usually very wide, therefore encouraging a greater dependence on foreign aid.

A common neoclassical argument for foreign private investment or foreign aid is that an inflow of foreign capital in the form of either of these two can, besides alleviating a significant portion of the deficit in the current account of the balance of payments, also help to remove that deficit over time if the foreign-owned enterprise can generate a net positive flow of export earnings or if the aid flows of financial resources are properly used to generate further revenue. Unfortunately for African countries, private capital, especially in the form of foreign private investment, moves towards the countries and regions with the highest financial returns and the greatest perceived safety, both of which are perceived by investors to be lacking in Africa. Equally unfortunate for Africa is that the availability of foreign aid discourages indigenous entrepreneurial initiative, weakening the necessity for these countries to outgrow aid dependency. The aid donors also use their economic power to influence the policies of recipient African governments in directions unfavourable for development. Often, they tie aid, especially soft loans, to their exports, as a result saddling the recipient African countries with substantial debt repayment burdens that exhaust their meagre development resources and further exacerbating their dependence on aid. . . .

The Benefits of Trade

Although international trade is believed to be characterised by unequal exchange between trading partners—an economic philosophy advocated by mercantilists during the seventeenth and eighteenth centuries, with [English economist] Thomas Munn at the forefront—it has nonetheless been acknowledged to generally enhance welfare and growth. According to [Scottish economist] Adam Smith's 1776 theory of absolute advantage a trading nation can gain by specialising in the production of the commodity of its absolute advantage and exchanging part of this output with other trading partners for the commodities of its absolute disadvantage. This process guarantees efficient use of resources, promotes productivity and increases in output and maximises welfare, all of which are considered dynamic gains from trade. Productivity and output increases, in particular, provide a measure of the gains from specialisation in production. Other positive derivatives include boosts in investments in innovations and technology. A limitation of the theory of absolute advantage, though, is that it alone cannot determine the pattern of trade. . . .

A Need to Diversify

The gains from world trade have increased several fold since the end of the Second World War in 1945, but continue to elude the African continent, especially the sub-Saharan countries, which often suffer shortages of essential commodities, implying the lack of international trade benefits. Africa's world export share, which was just 7.3 per cent in 1948, had by 2001 been reduced to less than half, reaching a low of about 1.5 per cent in 2004 for sub-Saharan Africa.

Arguments are many on the causes of Africa's poor trade performance. Some argue that the type of goods that Africans produce and export compared to the type they import has meant that the continent very often experiences deteriorating commodity terms of trade. These terms of trade deteriorate for a country if export prices decline relative to import prices, even though both may rise. The continuous decrease in the ratio of the prices of Africa's export commodities (comprising mainly primary commodities) to the prices of its imports (comprising mainly manufactured goods from developed countries) is argued to cost Africa a great deal. Table 1 shows that the selected countries, for which data are readily available, lost a total of $16.4 billion in 1990 alone, with Nigeria, the Ivory Coast, Gabon and Ghana having lost the most both in absolute terms and as a percentage of GDP. This development, which is due to the combined effects of low income and price elasticities of demand for primary commodities, is argued to continuously transfer income from Africa to the developed countries, resulting in Africa's poor growth in general. The low income and price elasticities of demand for Africa's commodities means that an increase in the supply of the commodities is accompanied by drastic price decreases that are unaccompanied by equally intense increases in demand, even with income growth in the importing developed countries.

Studies have revealed that a 1 per cent increase in developed country incomes will normally increase their imports of unprocessed foodstuffs and primary agricultural commodities (both the main exports of African countries) by a mere 0.6 per cent and 0.5 per cent, respectively. By contrast, the income elasticity of demand for manufactured commodities from developed countries is high, estimated at about 1.9 per cent. These estimates imply that commodities produced by Africans are treated as inferior goods. The real prices of primary products have reportedly decreased at an average annual rate of 0.6 per cent since 1900, implying that terms of trade have deteriorated over the decades. This would therefore mean that Africa's future trade prospects will continue to be bleak as long as the continent's exports remain concentrated on primary commodities and do not diversify significantly into manufactured and high-tech products.

Table 1: Terms of Trade Loss/Gain in Selected African Countries, 1990

Country	Index (baseline) 1980 = 100	Loss/(gain) $ million	Loss/(gain) as a % of GDP
Burkina Faso	98	3	0.0
Central African Rep.	94	8	0.6
Ghana	48	800	12.8
Kenya	75	344	3.9
Madagascar	85	59	1.9
Malawi	98	8	0.3
Mali	109	(29)	(1.2)
Mauritania	93	35	9.5
Niger	69	195	7.7
Nigeria	57	10,313	29.1
Rwanda	51	108	5.0
Sierra Leone	71	56	6.2
Tanzania	77	90	3.8
Togo	72	117	7.2
Uganda	55	124	4.1
Cameroon	63	704	6.3
Congo	70	484	16.9
Ivory Coast	62	1,594	16.1
Senegal	102	(15)	(0.3)
Gabon	63	1,451	30.1

Taken From: R.H. Green, *International Monetary and Financial Issues for the 1990s*, 1993.

Protectionist Barriers Stifle Diversification

It is also argued that the developed countries' protectionist trade policies cause a good deal of harm to African exports. For example, cotton subsidies in the USA and the under-priced cotton on the world market cost West African cotton producers and their economies an estimated US$250 million a year. The tariffs for low-priced African cocoa beans in the European Union (EU) are more or less nil, but increase to about 10 per cent for semi-processed cocoa and up to 30–50 per cent for the final product, chocolate, depending on the sugar and milk content. This means that tariff escalation penalises African producers when they add value. These tariffs suggest that both the EU and USA prefer that Africa should rather produce only unprocessed primary commodities, exposed to export earnings instability caused in part by low income and price elasticities of demand. The developed countries' protectionist policies also suggest that mercantilism, although since condemned, continues to be practised even in the twenty-first century. Other recent trade barriers include the arbitrarily imposed sanitary and phyto-sanitary rules that now form extra layers of developed country regulatory barriers, shutting out African exports. Having come into force in 1995 and officiously aimed at safeguarding human and animal health (through sanitary measures) and protecting plants from disease and pests (through phyto-sanitary measures), these rules have further limited the goods exported by many African countries to countries particularly within the Organisation for Economic Cooperation and Development (OECD). These rules, which demand certain standards, albeit set by the OECD member countries, are criticised as adding complex and intrusive regulations that burden many poor countries in Africa. . . .

Fostering Dependency on Aid

Africa's poor trade performance is also argued to be a result of insufficient investments aggravated by poor management and, most importantly, of the continent's refusal to outgrow its dependence on foreign aid. The continual management crises in Africa have meant that foreign aid to the continent has not been accompanied by trade reforms and capital investments to promote private capital flows and technology transfer. Rather, foreign aid has generally engendered a welfare mentality. This means that the continent continues to lack the technology to exploit its enormous wealth of resources or to influence the relative intensity with which its different factors of production can be used. Not even a populous and oil-resource-rich Nigeria has prioritised trade-boosting investments in infrastructure (roads, electricity and water), security, environmental protection and proper education. The country's existing roads are inadequate and often in poor condition because of poor maintenance and unruly traffic, power cuts are a daily occurrence, pure running water is non-existent and even the existing water facility is subject to the same supply failures as the power (electricity) facility. The majority of the country's cities are in a state of total environmental degradation and rendered unhealthy by filth, litter and rubbish-choked gutters. Equally serious are the generally poor security and a seriously deteriorating education system, both a by-product of decades of a militarised society.

These are not isolated problems unique to Nigeria, but actually widespread in Africa. For example, the problem of power cuts or an inadequate supply of electricity is also noted in countries such as Kenya, Cameroon, Egypt, Uganda, Tanzania, Senegal, the Democratic Republic of Congo (DRC), the Sudan and even a relatively affluent South Africa. Critics lament that this power shortfall remains a paradox considering that the continent is endowed with vast natural resources that could supply the deficiency. Interruptions of electricity and water supplies are very costly to manufacturing enterprise, since planning becomes more difficult, affecting production adversely and limiting growth potential. Good infrastructure is fundamental to decision making by investors: it creates the right environment for investment and industrial development. Apparently, creating such an environment is what most African governments are not doing. . . .

The often-common rhetoric from donors is that greater aid to Africa breeds corruption, implying that African institutions have a limited capacity to manage any substantial aid effectively. This frequently echoed sentiment is channelled to every sub-Saharan African country, including those that ordinarily may not need foreign aid. The sub-Saharan countries are perceived as the same by the rest of the world, especially in terms of culture, unsuitability for foreign investment and dependence on aid. According to the World Bank, sub-Saharan Africa is a high-cost, high-risk place to do business compared with other developing regions. The effect of this perceived unattractive business climate is that aid remains the largest source of external finance for countries in the region. One must wonder, though, how long Africa will remain dependent on foreign aid and what the continent should do to extricate itself from the 'aid trap'. . . .

Managing Resources

The outlook for resources remains positive in Africa, but the shortage of skills and technology continues to delay proper exploitation of the resources. Apparently, countries that have difficulty tapping their potential resources must rely largely on aid flows to fund development programmes, a description that has continued to fit African countries.

Africa hosts about 30 per cent of the world's mineral reserves, including 90 per cent of the platinum group of metals, 60 per cent of cobalt and 40 per cent of gold. Nigeria alone is the sixth biggest oil producer in the world and this suggests that, together with the other African oil producers, such as Libya, Angola, Equatorial Guinea and Gabon, the continent supplies a significant chunk of the total world oil requirements. This means that with proper resource management, through investment in skills and technology, a resource-rich Africa should be able to improve its international trade position, putting an end to the constant humiliating requests for foreign aid that have, through donor preferences and conditionality, continued to pressurise the recipient countries' government development plans. Critics argue that the conditionality imposed on aid-receiving countries has actually impaired the capacity of such countries to follow their own development routes of action. Apart from tying aid to donor countries' exports, as experienced by Ghana, other examples of donor aid-motivated influences include using aid funds to develop the donor's own managerial capacity to compete with host governments, especially for labour resources, as experienced by Mozambique and encouraging mushrooming non-governmental organisations, most of which distrust the host governments, often displaying hostile and dismissive attitudes by marginalising these governments' development efforts and preventing them from reaching a broader majority.

For African governments to shun aid will require setting up proper institutions to look after the interests of countries in the region, such institutions ushering in unambiguously interest politics, their most important goal being to succeed. An important move in this direction is the continental strategic development programme, called the New Partnership for Africa's Development (NEPAD), initiated by African leaders as a collective action to look into the region's economic problems in particular. The NEPAD, as a programme for building member countries' economic confidence and strength, should be successfully implemented through an economic integration of member countries. Through such integration the member states of an organisation can maximise their wealth and power. Integration promotes bigger markets that stimulate investments, promote specialisation and encourage competition among producers. It also leads to the creation of coordinated industrial planning, assigning given industries to different member countries, depending on the available local raw materials and thereby avoiding trade-diverting duplication of industries. Opportunities are created for industries to enjoy economies of scale of production. For consumers, the main associated benefits will include lower prices and a generally enhanced welfare because of the increased quantity and range of goods made available.

┃ *"African governments generally prefer*
┃ *... more aid and less accountability."*

Africa Needs Good Governance, Not Only Foreign Aid

Franklin Cudjoe

In the following viewpoint, Franklin Cudjoe asserts that more foreign aid is not the answer to Africa's economic woes. According to Cudjoe, aid often is misspent or stolen by corrupt governments that seek only to hold on to power. He maintains that African nations must be compelled to embrace good governance before any period of prosperity—whether through external aid or domestic entrepreneurship—can begin. Cudjoe, a Ghanaian by birth, is executive director of the Imani Center for Policy and Education and is pursuing a degree in public policy at Harvard University.

As you read, consider the following questions:

1. Why does Cudjoe believe that any development goals in Africa will not be met anytime soon?

2. As the author explains, how do Western aid advocates abet the never-ending charity model that corrupt African governments relish?

3. Despite rising aid packages, how many places did Ghana slip in the rankings of the World Bank's Doing Business Index in 2010, according to Cudjoe?

Heads of State from across the developing world arrived in New York last month [September 2010] for the annual United Nations meetings.

Heading up the agenda this year was a summit examining the UN Millennium Development Goals (MDGs) [targets for improving standards of living in developing nations].

These leaders—generally clad in expensive suits and heading enormous entourages—once again shamelessly moaned and complained over the lack of adequate progress on the MDGs, as if they and their governments were helpless bystanders in whether or not the MDGs are met.

Failed Aid Models Will Not Help Africa

There is nothing egregious about the eight MDG targets. Halving poverty, increasing education, and reducing maternal and child mortality are desirable outcomes. The only problem is that in the poorest countries, the goals will not be met because they are based on a failed development model of relying on external aid rather than internal policy change to facilitate economic development and growth.

And internal policy change is resisted fiercely by the very leaders expressing anguish over the lack of progress, because they and their cronies benefit richly from the current system, which focuses on securing foreign aid to be spent on thousands of carefully schemed but wasteful interventions in apparent pursuit of the MDGs. Such complex interventions, with little transparency and accountability on donor spending,

America Will Support Good Governance in Africa

America will not seek to impose any system of government on any other nation. The essential truth of democracy is that each nation determines its own destiny. But what America will do is increase assistance for responsible individuals and responsible institutions, with a focus on supporting good governance—on parliaments, which check abuses of power and ensure that opposition voices are heard; on the rule of law, which ensures the equal administration of justice: on civic participation, so that young people get involved; and on concrete solutions to corruption like forensic accounting and automating services strengthening hotlines, protecting whistle-blowers to advance transparency and accountability.

And we provide this support. I have directed my administration to give greater attention to corruption in our human rights reports. People everywhere should have the right to start a business or get an education without paying a bribe. We have a responsibility to support those who act responsibly and to isolate those who don't, and that is exactly what America will do.

Barack Obama,
Remarks to the Ghanaian Parliament,
Accra, July 11, 2009.

means few credible audits have been conducted on the billions of aid money spent over the years.

Governments That Steal and Plunder

Such expenditures have only served to entrench the very governments and policies that impede development.

African leaders in particular have been doing the math on how much they need to perpetuate their loot . . . um, I mean finance the MDGs. As the argument goes, "They ask why can't the rich Western countries provide $70 billion annually to meet the MDGs? It's only a fraction of their annual GDP [gross domestic product]. They can easily spare it, but it would mean so much in the developing world."

Western aid advocates do their part by painting gory pictures of famine and disease in Africa to justify the demand. Yet, African leaders have been able to squeeze close to $150 billion a year from their poor, developing countries to enrich themselves.

This figure didn't diminish even with the global financial crisis or following former Nigerian President Olusegun Obasanjo's admission of this habitual theft by African leaders and mock lamentation of corruption at the G-8 summit [a meeting of the eight wealthiest donor nations] in Gleneagles [Scotland] five years ago [in 2005].

In other words, African leaders have made a habit of stealing 25 per cent of the continent's GDP and squirreling it away for their own benefit. As if that is not enough, wasteful spending, legal plunder, prohibitive business environments and entrenched cronyism can be found even in Africa's most acclaimed democratic success stories such as Ghana.

More Aid, Less Growth

Ghana's democratic foundation is built on the politics of grand national development plans, which are presented to win voter support. These plans are largely sustained by aid, which demands little or no accountability.

Voters continually fall for promises by political parties that if elected, they will guide Ghana toward middle income status. These promises are slippery with target dates first of 2015, then 2020 and, doubtless, 2025 soon. Ghana has seen an increase in aid during the tenure of these political parties.

But the result has been depressing. Ghana slipped five places from (the 87th position to 92nd) on the World Bank's Doing Business 2010 Index and dropped in global competitiveness from 110th position in 2009 to 114th out of 139 countries in the 2010–2011 rankings by the World Economic Forum Global Competitiveness Index. At the MDG summit, German Chancellor Angela Merkel called for a balance between aid and good governance as a necessary condition for attaining the MDGs. Unfortunately, African governments generally prefer an imbalance with more aid and less accountability.

Donor nations need to understand this reality and get away from platitudes like the MDGs and aid targets and insist that African governments enact policies that will unleash the entrepreneurial spirits of Africans to create wealth and support national governments through taxation.

Aid may help governments that have already begun to tread this path, but providing ever-more aid in hopes that they will get richer only perpetuates the status quo.

| *"Africa is likely to get better with less meddling in its affairs by the West."*

Africa Will Progress Without Patronizing Interference from the West

Andrew M. Mwenda

In the following viewpoint, Andrew M. Mwenda claims that Western leaders are still chiding African nations for corruption and incompetence and offering stale models for change. Those outsiders, Mwenda insists, must come to terms with the fact that Africa is a diverse continent and that, like all nations, African countries will grow at their own speed. In the author's view, Western policies cannot and should not shape African progress; the needed change will come from Africans alone. Mwenda is the managing editor of the Ugandan newsmagazine The Independent.

As you read, consider the following questions:

1. According to Mwenda, what trite assumptions did President Obama make in his July 11, 2009, speech in Ghana?

2. As Mwenda states, the type of negotiated peace settlement that ended civil wars in Liberia and Sierra Leone would not have worked to resolve conflict in what other African nation?

3. Mwenda notes with irony that President Obama often uses what two nations as models of successful development?

On his recent visit to Ghana, U.S. President Barack Obama condemned war, corruption, tribalism, and all the other ills that have bedeviled our continent. Many Africans in Africa and the diaspora [people dispersed from an ancestral homeland] were moved by the speech [of July 11, 2009], as were many Africa observers in the West. The speech captivated imaginations because it appealed to people's basic common sense.

That is where its positive contribution ends.

Rather inconveniently, all the attention Obama's speech has gotten disproves his opening remark: "We must start from the simple premise that Africa's future is up to Africans." It is not the speech of an African leader on the future of the continent that is exciting debate in the media and finding space on the blogs; it is a speech by the U.S. president. This very simple contradiction reveals the world's collective tendency to seek Africa's solutions from the West.

Finding the Right Incentives for Change

Beyond its many good phrases and populist appeals, Obama's speech did not deviate fundamentally from the views of other Western leaders I have read throughout my lifetime—on aid, on civil wars, on corruption, or on democracy. Obama repackaged the same old views in less diplomatic language. He had the courage to be more explicit on Africa's ills because, due to his African heritage, Obama can say as he wishes without sounding racist—a fear that constrains other Western leaders when talking about Africa.

Even so, Obama said nothing new. He assumes that African countries have been mismanaged because leaders on the continent are bad men who make cold hearted choices. His solution is thus to extend moral pleas for them to rule better. Yet it is not the individual behavior of Africa's rulers that demands our closest attention, destructive as that behavior may be. It is the structure of incentives those leaders confront—incentives that help determine the choices they make.

Using this logic, we can start to ask more-useful questions. If the choices made by Africa's rulers have destroyed their economies, under what conditions can they develop a vested interest in growth-promoting policies? If Africans are going to war much more often than other human beings on the planet, what causes them to do so? When is peace more attractive than military combat?

No Single Blueprint for Success

Governing is not about making simplistic choices on who is right and who is wrong. It requires making complicated trade-offs, some of which might be costly in the short term. Take negotiated conflict settlements, for example, a policy that has stabilized Liberia and Sierra Leone after the two countries' brutal civil wars. That same policy wouldn't have worked in 1994 in Rwanda, where it would have produced an unstable power-sharing arrangement between victims of genocide and their executioners. The lesson: We cannot have one blueprint for all of Africa's problems. Even "good" moral decisions, such as those so often urged upon us by the West, can be bad sometimes.

Obama assumes that the fundamental challenge facing Africa is the lack of democracy and the checks and balances that come with it. But how does he explain why authoritarian Rwanda fights corruption and delivers public services to its citizens much better than its democratic neighbor, Uganda? In fact, the Ugandan brand of democracy has spawned corruption and incompetence more than it has helped combat them. The country's ethnic politics makes patronage and corruption more electorally profitable than delivering services.

Obama's preferred models of successful development, Singapore and South Korea, were not democratic when they rose to prominence. His proposals on ending corruption—"forensic accounting, automating services strengthening hot lines and protecting whistle-blowers"—are technocratic in nature. But the real challenge is how to give Africa's rulers a vested interest in fighting corruption. In most of Africa today, corruption is the way the system works—not the way it fails.

The lesson for Obama is that Africa is likely to get better with less meddling in its affairs by the West, not more—whether that meddling is through aid, peacekeeping, or well-written speeches. Africa needs space to make mistakes and learn from them. The solutions for Africa have to be shaped and articulated by Africans, not outsiders. Obama needs to listen to Africans much more, not lecture them using the same old teleprompter.

Periodical Bibliography

The following articles have been selected to supplement the diverse views presented in this chapter.

Douglas Alexander	"Trade and Aid Important for Africa," *New African*, January 2010.
George B.N. Ayittey	"Misleading Africa," *American Interest*, March/April 2009.
Thomas Cargill	"Party Over," *World Today*, June 2009.
Economist	"Promises, Promises," July 12, 2008.
Jonathan Glennie	"More Aid Is Not the Answer," *Current History*, May 2010.
Anne Jolis	"A Supply-Sider in East Africa," *Wall Street Journal*, April 24, 2010.
Joshua Kurlantzick	"Relief Disaster," *Mother Jones*, September/October 2008.
John Loxley and Harry A. Sackey	"Aid Effectiveness in Africa," *African Development Review*, September 2008.
Dambisa Moyo	"The Lure of Africa," *Economist World in 2010 Supplement*, November 21, 2009.
Dambisa Moyo	"Why Foreign Aid Is Hurting Africa," *Wall Street Journal*, March 21, 2009.
Kevin Peraino	"Sorry, Sudan," *Newsweek*, October 4, 2010.

OPPOSING
VIEWPOINTS®
SERIES

CHAPTER 3

What Is the State of the AIDS Epidemic in Africa?

Chapter Preface

According to the Joint United Nations Programme on AIDS/HIV (UNAIDS) *Global Report 2010*, the number of people in the world living with the human immunodeficiency virus (HIV)—which includes those who suffer from acquired immune deficiency syndrome (AIDS)—was 33,300,000 in 2009. Of that staggering number of individuals, 22,500,000 resided in sub-Saharan Africa. The country of South Africa alone was home to 5,600,000 people living with HIV/AIDS. Nigeria had an estimated 3,300,000 HIV carriers; while Kenya, Mozambique, Uganda, Tanzania, and Zimbabwe each had more than 1 million infected citizens. Although some sub-Saharan African nations witnessed declines in infection rates in 2009, UNAIDS reports that the majority of new HIV infections occurred in the region (1.6 to 2.2 million cases).

Despite the good news that incidence rates have been falling in 22 sub-Saharan countries, UNAIDS affixes the blame for continued HIV transmission in the region on three major causes: intravenous drug use, men having unprotected sex with other men, and prostitution. The first of these causes is a relatively new phenomenon in sub-Saharan countries, the organization contends, but a growing concern. UNAIDS claims that available data suggest more than one-third of admitted injected-drug users in Nairobi, Kenya, for example, tested positive for HIV. Furthermore, in some countries such as Mauritius (which reports 8,800 HIV/AIDS sufferers), the main pathway of transmission has been through intravenous drug use.

Prostitution and men having sex with men remain major avenues of HIV transmission in sub-Saharan Africa chiefly because of the high incidence of unprotected sex. UNAIDS maintains that 32 percent of new HIV cases in Ghana result from paid sex, while 20 percent of new cases in Senegal and 15 percent of new cases in Rwanda and Kenya can be attributed to men having sex with men. The latter is a concern for health workers because many men who have sex with other men also have sex with women, thus increasing chances of both homosexual and heterosexual transmission of the virus.

To counter these worrisome trends in HIV infection, UN-AIDS, the World Health Organization, and other AIDS-activism groups have tried to increase education about the disease and distribute condoms and antiretroviral drugs in the region. Making more people aware of the risks of transmission as well as the safeguards of condom use has achieved some impressive results. UNAIDS reports, for instance, that the number of children born with the virus declined by 32 percent between 2004 and 2009. The organization also attests that 37 percent of HIV/AIDS patients in the region were receiving antiretroviral drugs and that these powerful therapies were helping recipients live longer, more productive lives.

In the following chapter, several experts discuss the extent of the HIV/AIDS crisis in Africa and the factors that may be contributing to its spread. While some are optimistic about thwarting—and possibly curing—the disease, others remain concerned that not enough is being done to save the continent from the ravages of the killer virus.

> *"Although both international and do-mestic efforts to overcome the crisis have been strengthened in recent years, the people of sub-Saharan Africa will continue to feel the effects of HIV and AIDS for many years to come."*

AIDS Is a Serious Threat in Africa

AVERT

In the following viewpoint, AVERT argues that AIDS is still widespread in Africa, killing millions each year. The organization states that AIDS is destroying families, straining economies, and taxing health care services. According to AVERT, AIDS is erasing African nations' progress in reducing infant mortality and in building stronger markets. AVERT maintains that the only way to effectively fight the disease is to understand how its transmission is linked to other social problems such as poverty and lack of health services. AVERT is an international HIV and AIDS charity based in the United Kingdom. It seeks to provide information about the spread and impact of the disease and to speed treatment to those affected.

As you read, consider the following questions:

1. According to AVERT, how much of a family's monthly income might be consumed in taking care of a family member with AIDS?

2. As the author reports, how many more times likely is it that a young person with no education will contract AIDS in sub-Saharan Africa?

3. According to a study cited by AVERT, by what percentage could a company's profits be cut due to AIDS-related absenteeism, productivity loss, health care costs, and recruitment of new employees?

Two-thirds of all people infected with HIV live in sub-Saharan Africa, although this region contains little more than 10% of the world's population. AIDS has caused immense human suffering in the continent. The most obvious effect of this crisis has been illness and death, but the impact of the epidemic has certainly not been confined to the health sector; households, schools, workplaces and economies have also been badly affected.

During 2009 alone, an estimated 1.3 million adults and children died as a result of AIDS in sub-Saharan Africa. Since the beginning of the epidemic more than 15 million Africans have died from AIDS.

Although access to antiretroviral treatment is starting to lessen the toll of AIDS, fewer than half of Africans who need treatment are receiving it. The impact of AIDS will remain severe for many years to come.

The Impact on the Health Sector

In all heavily affected countries the AIDS epidemic is adding additional pressure on the health sector. As the epidemic matures, the demand for care for those living with HIV rises, as does the toll of AIDS on health workers.

As the HIV prevalence of a country rises, the strain placed on its hospitals is likely to increase. In sub-Saharan Africa, people with HIV-related diseases occupy more than half of all hospital beds. Government-funded research in South Africa has suggested that, on average, HIV-positive patients stay in hospital four times longer than other patients.

Hospitals are struggling to cope, especially in poorer African countries where there are often too few beds available. This shortage results in people being admitted only in the later stages of illness, reducing their chances of recovery.

While AIDS is causing an increased demand for health services, large numbers of healthcare professionals are being directly affected by the epidemic. Botswana, for example, lost 17% of its healthcare workforce due to AIDS between 1999 and 2005. A study in one region of Zambia found that 40% of midwives were HIV-positive. Healthcare workers are already scarce in most African countries. Excessive workloads, poor pay and migration to richer countries are among the factors contributing to this shortage.

Although the recent increase in the provision of antiretroviral drugs (which significantly delay the progression from HIV to AIDS) has brought hope to many in Africa, it has also put increased strain on healthcare workers. Providing antiretroviral treatment to everyone who needs it requires more time and training than is currently available in most countries.

The Impact on Households

The toll of HIV and AIDS on households can be very severe. Although no part of the population is unaffected by HIV, it is often the poorest sectors of society that are most vulnerable to the epidemic and for whom the consequences are most severe. In many cases, the presence of AIDS causes the household to dissolve, as parents die and children are sent to relatives for care and upbringing. A study in rural South Africa suggested that households in which an adult had died from AIDS were four times more likely to dissolve than those in which no deaths had occurred. Much happens before this dissolution takes place: AIDS strips families of their assets and income earners, further impoverishing the poor.

In Botswana it is estimated that, on average, every income earner is likely to acquire one additional dependent over the next ten years due to the AIDS epidemic. A dramatic increase in destitute households—those with no income earners—is also expected.

Other countries in the region are experiencing the same problem, as individuals who would otherwise provide a household with income are prevented from working—either because they are ill with AIDS themselves or because they are caring for another sick family member.

Such a situation is likely to have repercussions for every member of the family. Children may be forced to abandon their education and in some cases women may be forced to turn to sex work. This can lead to a higher risk of HIV transmission, which further exacerbates the situation.

A study in South Africa found that poor households coping with members who are sick from HIV or AIDS were reducing spending on necessities even further. The most likely expenses to be cut were clothing (21%), electricity (16%) and other services (9%). Falling incomes forced about 6% of households to reduce the amount they spent on food and almost half of households reported having insufficient food at times.

The AIDS epidemic adds to food insecurity in many areas, as agricultural work is neglected or abandoned due to household illness. In Malawi, where food shortages have had a devastating effect, it has been recognised that HIV and AIDS have diminished the country's agricultural output. It was calculated in 2006 that by 2020, Malawi's agricultural workforce will be 14% smaller than it would have been without HIV and AIDS.

In other countries, such as Mozambique, Botswana, Namibia and Zimbabwe, the reduction is likely to be over 20%.

A study in Kenya demonstrated that food production in households in which the head of the family died of AIDS were affected in different ways depending on the sex of the deceased. As in other sub-Saharan African countries, it was generally found that the death of a male reduced the production of 'cash crops' (such as coffee, tea and sugar), while the death of a female reduced the production of grain and other crops necessary for household survival.

Taking care of a person sick with AIDS is not only an emotional strain for household members, but also a major strain on household resources. Loss of income, additional care-related expenses, the reduced ability of caregivers to work, and mounting medical fees push affected households deeper into poverty. It is estimated that, on average, HIV-related care can absorb one-third of a household's monthly income.

The financial burden of death can also be considerable, with some families in South Africa easily spending seven times their total household monthly income on a funeral. Furthermore, although many South Africans contribute to some sort of funeral insurance plan, many of these are inadequately funded, and it is arguable that such financial arrangements detract from other savings plans or health insurance.

Aside from the financial burden, providing home based care can impose demands on the physical, mental and general health of carers—usually family and friends of the sick person. Such risks are amplified if carers are untrained or unsupported by a home-based care organisation. . . .

The Impact on Children

It is hard to overemphasise the trauma and hardship that children affected by HIV and AIDS are forced to bear. The epidemic not only causes children to lose their parents or guardians, but sometimes their childhood as well.

As parents and family members become ill, children take on more responsibility to earn an income, produce food, and care for family members. It is harder for these children to access adequate nutrition, basic health care, housing and clothing.

Because AIDS claims the lives of people at an age when most already have young children, more children have been orphaned by AIDS in Africa than anywhere else. Many children are now raised by their extended families and some are even left on their own in child-headed households.

As projections of the number of AIDS orphans rise, some have called for an increase in institutional care for children. However this solution is not only expensive but also detrimental to the children. Institutionalisation stores up problems for society, which is ill equipped to cope with an influx of young adults who have not been socialised in the community in which they have to live. There are alternatives available. One example is the approach developed by church groups in Zimbabwe, in which community members are recruited to visit orphans in their homes, where they live either with foster parents, grandparents or other relatives, or in child-headed households.

The way forward is prevention. Firstly, it is crucial to prevent children from becoming infected with HIV at birth as well as later in life. Secondly, if efforts are made to prevent adults becoming infected with HIV, and to care for those already infected, then fewer children will be orphaned by AIDS in the future.

The Impact on the Education Sector

The relationship between AIDS and the education sector is circular—as the epidemic worsens, the education sector is damaged, which in turn is likely to increase the incidence of HIV transmission. There are numerous ways in which AIDS can affect education, but equally there are many ways in which

Lesotho: A Country Nearly Destroyed by AIDS

Since the first case of AIDS illness in Lesotho was recorded in 1986, in the windswept mountain district of Mokhotlong, the disease has spread rapidly throughout the country [which has a population of roughly 2.1 million]. While at first HIV infection was more common among foreigners and commercial sex workers and their clients, today the majority of those infected have no easily identifiable risk behaviour. Adult HIV prevalence rose from 4% in 1993, to 9.8% in 1998, to 31% in 2002. . . . Lesotho is now ... among the top five countries in the world in terms of level of HIV infections. Nearly half the women receiving antenatal care in Maseru, the capital city, are infected with HIV, and a person in Lesotho who turns 15 years old today has a 74% chance of becoming infected before age 50. At least 15% of babies born each year are HIV-positive, and there are more than 97,000 children orphaned by AIDS, most of whom are of unknown serostatus [disease status]. Before the onset of the epidemic, life expectancy had been projected to increase to 60 years by 2003; now it has drastically declined to 44 years for women and 39 years for men.

David A. Himmelgreen et al.,
African Journal of AIDS Research, *2009.*

education can help the fight against AIDS. The extent to which schools and other education institutions are able to continue functioning will influence how well societies eventually recover from the epidemic.

A decline in school enrolment is one of the most visible effects of the epidemic. This in itself will have an effect on

HIV prevention, as a good, basic education ranks among the most effective and cost-effective means of preventing HIV.

There are numerous barriers to school attendance in Africa. Children may be removed from school to care for parents or family members, or they may themselves be living with HIV. Many are unable to afford school fees and other such expenses—this is particularly a problem among children who have lost their parents to AIDS, who often struggle to generate income.

Studies have suggested that young people with little or no education may be around twice as likely to contract HIV as those who have completed primary education. In this context, the devastating effect that AIDS is having on school enrolment is a big concern. In Swaziland and the Central African Republic, it was reported that school enrolment fell by 25–30% due to AIDS at the beginning of the millennium.

HIV and AIDS are having a devastating effect on the already inadequate supply of teachers in African countries; for example, a study in South Africa found that 21% of teachers aged 25–34 were living with HIV.

Teachers who are affected by HIV and AIDS are likely to take periods of time off work. Those with sick families may also take time off to attend funerals or to care for sick or dying relatives, and further absenteeism may result from the psychological effects of the epidemic. . . .

The Impact on Enterprises and Workplaces

HIV and AIDS dramatically affect labour, setting back economic and social progress. The vast majority of people living with HIV in Africa are between the ages of 15 and 49—in the prime of their working lives.

AIDS damages businesses by squeezing productivity, adding costs, diverting productive resources, and depleting skills. Company costs for health-care, funeral benefits and pension fund commitments are likely to rise as the number of people taking early retirement or dying increases. Also, as the impact of the epidemic on households grows more severe, market demand for products and services can fall. The epidemic hits productivity through increased absenteeism. Comparative studies of East African businesses have shown that absenteeism can account for as much as 25–54% of company costs.

A study in several Southern African countries has estimated that the combined impact of AIDS-related absenteeism, productivity declines, health-care expenditures, and recruitment and training expenses could cut profits by at least 6–8%. Another study of a thousand companies in Southern Africa found that 9% had suffered a significant negative impact due to AIDS. In areas that have been hit hardest by the epidemic, it found that up to 40% of companies reported that HIV and AIDS were having a negative effect on profits. . . .

Reversing Gains

In many countries of sub-Saharan Africa, AIDS is erasing decades of progress in extending life expectancy. In the worst affected countries, average life expectancy has fallen by twenty years because of the epidemic. Life expectancy at birth in Swaziland is just 31 years—less than half of what it would be without AIDS.

The impact that AIDS has had on average life expectancy is partly attributed to child mortality, as increasing numbers of babies are born with HIV infections acquired from their mothers. The biggest increase in deaths, however, has been among adults aged between 20 and 49 years. This group now accounts for 60% of all deaths in sub-Saharan Africa, compared to 20% between 1985 and 1990, when the epidemic was in its early stages. By affecting this age group so heavily, AIDS is hitting adults in their most economically productive years and removing the very people who could be responding to the crisis.

Through its impacts on the labour force, households and enterprises, AIDS has played a significant role in the reversal of human development in Africa. One aspect of this development reversal has been the damage that the epidemic has done to the economy, which, in turn, has made it more difficult for countries to respond to the crisis.

One way in which AIDS affects the economy is by reducing the labour supply through increased mortality and illness. Amongst those who are able to work, productivity is likely to decline as a result of HIV-related illness. Government income also declines, as tax revenues fall and governments are pressured to increase their spending to deal with the expanding HIV epidemic.

The abilities of African countries to diversify their industrial base, expand exports and attract foreign investment are integral to economic progress in the region. By making labour more expensive and reducing profits, AIDS limits the ability of African countries to attract industries that depend on low-cost labour and makes investments in African businesses less desirable.

The impact that AIDS has had on the economies of African countries is difficult to measure. The economies of the worst affected countries were already struggling with development challenges, debt and declining trade before the epidemic started to affect the continent. AIDS has combined with these factors to further aggravate the situation. It is thought that the impact of AIDS on the gross domestic product (GDP) of the worst affected countries is a loss of around 1.5% per year; this means that after 25 years the economy would be 31% smaller than it would otherwise have been.

An Ongoing Crisis

This [viewpoint] has outlined just some of the ways in which the AIDS epidemic has had a significant impact on countries in sub-Saharan Africa. Although both international and domestic efforts to overcome the crisis have been strengthened in recent years, the people of sub-Saharan Africa will continue to feel the effects of HIV and AIDS for many years to come. It is clear that as much as possible needs to be done to minimise this impact.

As access to treatment is slowly expanded throughout the continent, millions of lives are being extended and hope is being given to people who previously had none. Unfortunately though, the majority of people in need of treatment are still not receiving it, and campaigns to prevent new infections (which must remain the central focus of the fight against AIDS) are lacking in many areas.

The impact of AIDS in Africa is linked to many other problems, such as poverty and poor public infrastructures. Efforts to fight the epidemic must take these realities into account, and look at ways in which the general development of Africa can progress. As the evidence discussed in this [viewpoint] makes clear, however, AIDS is acting as a serious barrier to Africa's development. Much wider access to HIV prevention, treatment and care services is urgently needed.

| *"[UNAIDS] has grossly exaggerated the world AIDS threat."*

The Threat of AIDS in Africa Has Been Overstated

Michael Fumento

In the following viewpoint, Michael Fumento argues that the number of AIDS cases in Africa, and around the world, have been greatly overstated. In some cases, the exaggeration may be totally unrealistic, Fumento states, and even concocted for advocacy purposes. He maintains that the pretense of a huge AIDS epidemic detracts spending from curable ailments, such as malaria and tuberculosis. Michael Fumento is a senior fellow at the Hudson Institute in Washington, DC, and a nationally syndicated columnist for Scripps Howard News Service.

As you read, consider the following questions:

1. How, according to the author, has UNAIDS "grossly exaggerated" the world AIDS threat?

2. How does Fumento respond to Bill Clinton's statement, "It's difficult to imagine how the world can grow unless we tackle AIDS"?

3. What does Fumento refer to as "the AIDS industry"?

Calls for prevention highlighted the opening day of the 16th International AIDS Conference in Toronto last week [mid-August 2006]. Alas, it's too late. On the same day the *Washington Post*, carried a photo on its front page depicting a man wearing a T-shirt reading: "We all have AIDS." Toss out those condoms; forget abstinence, and don't bother getting tested. Or what part of "all" don't you understand?

We Do Not All Have AIDS

Seriously, this bit of propaganda is but one illustration of how efforts against AIDS have always been handicapped by politics. Nobody really believes we all have AIDS. But many have bought into the "Everyone is at risk" nonsense, which clearly works against targeting those truly at risk. The entire science of epidemiology—which began when London physician John Snow mapped out cholera cases in his city and found they clustered around a single water pump—depends on identifying risk factors to ameliorate them. In Snow's case, he simply removed the pump handle and the epidemic ended.

He was lucky he didn't have to deal with activists carrying signs reading: "Water doesn't cause cholera; ignorance and prejudice cause cholera!"

Since 1985, when *Life* magazine blared in huge red letters: "Now No One Is Safe from AIDS," activists have fought furiously against the idea that AIDS targets those who engage in selective behaviors. Yet over two decades later AIDS remains in this country overwhelmingly a disease of homosexual males and intravenous drug users. Fewer than 39,000 Americans were diagnosed with AIDS in 2004 (latest data available), and fewer than 16,000 died from it. That's about one in 770 and one in 1,875 respectively. Fact is, almost *everybody* is safe from AIDS.

But of course, the focus of this conference is on international AIDS, which we all know is wiping whole continents off the map. A high Ugandan official said that within two years his nation will "be a desert." ABC News' *Nightline* declared that within 12 years "50 million Africans may have died of AIDS."

Problem is, those predictions were made in 1986 and 1988. Yet since 1985, Uganda's population has fully doubled. *Nightline*'s 50 million dead by the year 2000 proved to be 20 million in 2005, according to the UN's estimate. Further, "In sub-Saharan Africa, the region with the largest burden of the AIDS epidemic, data also indicate that the HIV incidence rate has peaked in most countries," according to the 2006 UNAIDS Report.

Ensuring an Epidemic

These figures are from an agency that itself has grossly exaggerated the world AIDS threat. For example, in 1998 it estimated that 12% of Rwandans age 15–49 were infected; now it says it's only 3%. Whoops. On the other hand, other agencies had estimated a horrific 30% of Rwandans were infected. According to James Chin, a former U.N. official who made some of the earliest global HIV estimates, such concocted figures are "pure advocacy."

Yet former President Bill Clinton told conference attendees that "It's difficult to imagine how the world can grow unless we tackle AIDS." In fact world population growth is fastest in areas hardest hit by AIDS.

As for the bizarre assertion that AIDS remains yet to be tackled, UNAIDS reports that 1.3 million people in low- and middle-income countries received antiretroviral therapy in 2004, up from a fifth that number in 2001. Donated blood is now screened in even the poorest countries. The level of AIDS testing and education in poorer nations has skyrocketed.

Consequences of an Overstated Threat

Meanwhile, worldwide AIDS spending averaged $1.7 billion between 2002–2004 but reached $8.3 billion for 2005 and is slated to hit $10 billion in 2007. The size of that pie, and the desire to have a slice of it, is all you need to know to understand how the Toronto conference could attract a stunning 24,000 attendees who have been rightly labeled "the AIDS industry." Nevertheless, insists UNAIDS, that $10 billion isn't nearly enough.

No matter that even the current AIDS budget swamps spending on malaria and tuberculosis [TB], which together kill about twice as many people annually as does AIDS. Antiretroviral therapy for AIDS cures no one and while it costs relatively little in the Third World—$300–$1,200 per year— compared to North America, TB can be cured with $65 of medicine. Malaria in Africa and Asia can be prevented for a pittance by spraying [the pesticide] DDT, yet environmental activists and the European Union have essentially blocked its use in those areas that need it most.

Alas for these victims, they don't have a politically correct disease. And for that they must die.

> *"Failure to emphasize macro-social factors . . . remains a major barrier in the war against HIV/AIDS."*

Social and Economic Factors Contribute to the Spread of AIDS in Africa

Ben Wodi

In the following viewpoint, Ben Wodi claims that many strategies in the fight against AIDS in Africa focus on the supposedly unrestrained behaviors of the African people. Wodi insists that this attitude neglects the underlying causes of certain behaviors. Thus, he argues that in order to fight AIDS, African countries and international agencies must address socioeconomic factors such as poverty, lack of education, poor health services, and the patriarchal structure of marriage in many African communities. Wodi contends that these forces are chiefly to blame for the spread of AIDS and should be rectified through targeted aid, more effective government leadership, and better education. Wodi is a professor of health and the coordinator of international programs in health at the State University of New York at Cortland.

Ben Wodi, "Re-evaluating Socioeconomic Conditions and the Continuing Spread of HIV/AIDS in Sub-Saharan Africa," *Western Journal of Black Studies*, vol. 29, no. 2, 2005. pp. 521–531. All rights reserved. Reproduced by permission.

As you read, consider the following questions:

1. At the Kenyan town hall meeting referenced by the author, what did the participants identify as factors contributing to the spread of HIV/AIDS in their region?

2. According to Wodi, why are sub-Saharan African women less likely to be influenced by media campaigns spreading AIDS awareness?

3. As Wodi reports, of the $1 billion fund introduced in Zimbabwe to fight AIDS, what percentage actually was allocated to health programs? What happened to the rest of the money?

The ravages of the HIV/AIDS pandemic in sub-Saharan Africa are widely acknowledged. The unique challenges in combating the spread of the disease in the region have also been widely discussed. While a number of well meaning individuals and organizations continue to find ways to reduce the morbidity and mortality rates of the disease in the region, socioeconomic (as well as political) factors remain major constraints in this effort. For example, many governments in the region are yet to fully acknowledge HIV/AIDS as a major cause of morbidity and mortality in their vital statistics for fear of the stigma associated with the disease including economic consequences. Those that do are disappointed with the limited support provided by the rich nations of the world for combating the disease in the region. Many African leaders are suspicious of the real intentions of individuals and organizations from affluent countries on the premise that they focus more on behavior and morality rather than socioeconomic factors.

Blaming Behavior

The behavioral and biological risk factors in the etiology [the study of causation or origination] of HIV/AIDS in Africa have been widely discussed with most researchers focusing on the behavioral aspects of the disease. Conspicuously limited in these discussions is the role of socioeconomic factors. [Medical history writers Randall M.] Packard and [Paul] Epstein have criticized the association of Africans with sexual promiscuity and the tendency of Western thought to link sexuality with high incidence of HIV/AIDS in Africa. The focus on micro-social factors such as African sexuality and culture in communicable disease etiology dates back in Western thought. "Is the attitude of medical researchers towards AIDS in Africa not based on a deeply embedded image or trope which continues to shape western and popular thought about African sexuality?" the above authors question. The emphasis on behavioral factors in the spread of HIV/AIDS in sub-Saharan Africa would appear to mask the socioeconomic conditions that fuel the pandemic in the first place. Failure to emphasize macro-social factors such as economic impoverishment, access to education, especially educational empowerment of women, access to health care, man-made and natural disasters among others, remains a major barrier in the war against HIV/AIDS. The need to understand the political and socioeconomic context within which these behavioral factors occur is of particular significance in the region and would avert victim blaming. . . .

Looking at Socioeconomic Factors

As stated earlier, the focus on the sexual behavior of sub-Saharan Africans would appear to ignore those socioeconomic conditions that produce the epidemic in the first place. An important question worth addressing is why a disease like HIV/AIDS follows a different epidemiological pattern in Africa compared to western countries. The answer is rooted in the historical, political, economic and of course sociocultural environments. In the case of Africa, [sociological anthropologist Ann] Akeroyd notes how the traditional family, social, and

environmental structures were disrupted by European hege-
monic adventures. Adjustment of Africans to the ensuing
changes cannot be ignored in the behaviors that predispose
them to the contagion. Packard and Epstein present a stronger
argument for viewing Africans as victims of HIV/AIDS. The
authors liken HIV/AIDS research in Africa to earlier studies
on syphilis and tuberculosis in which Africans were clearly
blamed for the more virulent epidemiologic pattern that these
diseases followed in the region. Earlier assumptions about
syphilis and tuberculosis epidemiology focused on behavioral
theories rather than socioeconomic [factors]. Focusing on the
socioeconomic contexts in the epidemiology of HIV/AIDS in
Africa would allow for "open ended discussion of a wide range
of social, political and economic conditions which may be affecting health levels in Africa . . ." rather than "placing responsibility for transmission on the actors themselves in a not too
subtle form of victim blaming," the above authors conclude.
In other words, the disease should be seen as a human rights
issue rather than a damning condemnation of its victims.
[Medical anthropologist Didien] Fassin and [former director
of the Center for Health Policy Study at the University of Wit-
waters in South Africa Helen] Schneider advocate another approach to discussing the spread of HIV/AIDS within the political economy as well as political anthropology. They argue
for a coherent social epidemiology in scientific studies of
HIV/AIDS in Africa citing social inequalities and employment
status as powerful predictors of susceptibility to HIV.

Kenya has one of the highest HIV/AIDS disease burdens
in Africa. At a town hall meeting conducted by this author in
Kenya in 2002, participants were queried about their opinions
regarding the causes of the high caseload of HIV/AIDS in that
country. Although not a representative sample of the Kenyan
population, participants were from various institutions of
higher learning as well as activist and philanthropic organizations. The responses were similar to the arguments presented

above and centered on the need to emphasize those socioeconomic conditions that fuel the spread of the disease in Kenya. Participants identified unemployment/poverty, migrant labor, limited educational opportunities, limited political will, limited access to condoms, the low status of women, the slow reaction of the international community and other sociocultural correlates in HIV/AIDS epidemiology in that country. Interestingly, most of these conditions are similar to those that chart the course of the pandemic in other parts of Africa, especially south of the Sahara. . . .

Economic Dependence of Women

Among sub-Saharan Africans, women have become a particular class of victims of the HIV/AIDS pandemic. The impact of the low status of women in patriarchal societies relative to the spread of HIV/AIDS has been widely discussed. Participants in the aforementioned town hall meeting also identified the low status of women in Kenya as a major factor in the spread of HIV/AIDS in the country. They cited women's limited ability to negotiate safe sex in a male-dominated society as a major obstacle to controlling the incidence of the contagion. Studies continue to show that women bear a disproportionate burden of those infected, as they constitute 58% of the disease burden in the region. Adolescent girls are 3–4 times more likely to be infected compared to their male counterparts. The patriarchal nature of African societies continues to shape women's sexual behavior in the region. This in turn accounts for the high prevalence of HIV/AIDS among women in sub-Saharan Africa. Of the several factors implicated in the unequal prevalence of the disease among women in Africa, economic dependency/feminization of poverty, unequal distribution of sexual power (sexual violence and coercion), limited educational opportunities and lack of political will, continue to dominate the literature. . . .

Several social, economic, political and other factors account for African women's dependence on men and their consequent vulnerability to HIV/AIDS. In African societies, the desire by men to have many children and women to validate their marriage through multiparity, have been implicated in the spread of this contagion. . . . Compared to Western countries, women in traditional African societies lack the power to deny sex to their spouses even when they can prove instances of marital infidelity in their relationship. . . .

Gender inequity in health care remains another factor in the disproportionate burden of HIV/AIDS among women in sub-Saharan Africa. Women are less likely to seek health care or be cared for in health care settings compared to men. Socioeconomic status and low literacy are major factors influencing this outcome. Low literacy rates tend to hamper women's knowledge about prevention strategies. Many women in the region are less likely to benefit from anti-HIV/AIDS campaigns channeled through the print media. Men mostly own radios and televisions. Women in rural settings are worse off in this regard. Women are more likely to delay seeking health care either because symptoms were not considered severe, had disappeared or for lack of money. Even when women sought care, they were more likely than their male counterparts to turn to public health care facilities where marginal care is the norm. . . .

Poverty, Unemployment, and HIV/AIDS

Unemployment, underemployment and consequent poverty continue to account for the high incidence of HIV/AIDS in Africa. Abject poverty in sub-Saharan Africa is the norm. In 1996, the average Gross National Product per capita for industrialized nations was $27,086.00 compared to $528.00 among African Nations. This would indicate a 51-fold disparity in wealth. In Africa where the richest 20 percent of the population controls the wealth, economic survival overrides other life decisions among the poor thus accounting for self-fulfilling prophecy (victim blaming) in their susceptibility to disease. Unless poverty is alleviated along with other political and social constraints, one can expect little progress in controlling HIV/AIDS as well as its consequences in this region of the world.

The relationship between poverty and HIV/AIDS has been widely discussed in the literature. Using the [United Nations] Human Development Index [HDI], which includes life expectancy at birth, adult literacy, gross enrollment ratio, and per capita economic production, [African health expert Josef] Decosas notes an inverse relationship between HDI scores and HIV/AIDS. While Canada ranked first at 0.95 in 1995, Niger ranked last at 0.207. Most countries in sub-Saharan Africa ranked low on this measurement scale. Clearly, while the prevalence of HIV can slow development, lack of development can also foster an increase in HIV. . . .

Effects of Politics on HIV/AIDS

Commitment at the highest level of leadership among nations in Africa is part of the recipe needed to begin reversing the HIV/AIDS trend in the region. After years of lethargy and denial about the scope of the HIV/AIDS epidemic in sub-Saharan Africa, it is heartening to know that many leaders in the region are now recognizing the disease as a national emergency. As noted earlier, Uganda in East Africa continues to be applauded for their government's unequivocal commitment to the control of HIV. A significant decline in incidence of the disease in that country has been continuously recorded since 1993. Similar government campaigns against HIV/AIDS in Zambia, Senegal and more recently Botswana are showing some progress albeit painfully slow. . . .

After President [Thabo] Mbeki's political furor stating that HIV does not cause AIDS [a belief he espoused in the early 2000s], he is finally playing a leadership role in the control of

HIV transmission in South Africa. It took a court order from the Constitutional Court to get him to make antiretroviral drugs such as nevirapine available to pregnant women in order to prevent mother-to-child transmission. In Zimbabwe, [journalist Khabir] Ahmad notes the dissolution of the AIDS Council Board because of political infighting. As a result of the fact that 25 percent of the population in Zimbabwe is seropositve for HIV, the government introduced a 3 percent levy culminating in a $1 billion fund to help fight the disease. This action was lauded by health care providers only to be plagued by political loyalty and mismanagement. Only 15 percent of the fund was actually allocated to HIV/AIDS programs while the rest was believed to have been diverted to fund defense and military projects. This is typical of how well-meaning projects in the region fall victim to politics thus exacerbating numerous health conditions.

However, several African leaders have begun to show commitment by directly presiding on HIV/AIDS commissions. Burkina Faso, Burundi, Congo, Ethiopia, Ghana, Kenya, Mozambique, Niger, and Nigeria are examples of countries whose presidents and Prime Ministers have shown commitment at the highest level of leadership by directly presiding over HIV/AIDS commissions. A United Nations Special Session on HIV/AIDS in June 2001 stated, "Strong leadership at all levels of society is essential for an effective response to the epidemic. Leadership by governments in combating HIV/AIDS is essential and their efforts should be complemented by the full and active participation of civil society, the business community and private sector. Leadership involves personal commitment and concrete actions." The leadership among sub-Saharan heads of state cited above is consistent with the one advocated in the aforementioned United Nations Special Session and must be sustained if significant decline in incidence of this scourge is to be achieved.

The International Community Must Act

The role of the international community in the war against HIV/AIDS cannot be overstated. Lessons in epidemiology would suggest that early intervention to limit spread and to break the web of causation remain very vital in the war against HIV/AIDS. This is a signal for the international community, especially donor countries and agencies to aggressively infuse resources at this time rather than later when the cost will be greater socioeconomically. The Director-General of the World Health Organization estimated in 2002 that investing $3.40 for each person at risk would make a significant impact in the spread of HIV/AIDS globally compared to the current funding of only 40 cents.

The need for the International Monetary Fund [IMF], The World Bank, and other International Financial Institutions to engage on a program of debt relief for HIPCs [heavily indebted poor countries] has been argued extensively. In 2003, UNAIDS [the Joint United Nations Programme on HIV/AIDS] noted that "The debts of 38 highly indebted poor countries (HIPC) amount on the average, to more than four times their annual export earnings. These debt servicing obligations can undermine a country's social spending, including that required for HIV/AIDS and orphan responses." It helps to know that IMF and World Bank are cognizant of this. They are increasingly more willing to provide debt relief to some HIPCs. However, this must not be tied to the structural adjustment program of the early 1980's that forced many poor African countries to introduce austere measures aimed at cost recovery. Such cost recovery efforts only created huge socioeconomic disparities and deepened poverty among the disenfranchised, especially educational opportunities. Free universal education throughout sub-Sahara Africa is important in the war against HIV/AIDS and is now well advocated.

Several programs targeted at sub-Saharan Africa, if sustained and simplified, will continue to make a difference. For example, the international community has hailed commitment of $15 billion dollars by the United States government over the next five years towards the fight against HIV/AIDS in sub-Saharan Africa and the Caribbean as an effort in the right direction. However, the program appears to be punctuated with a lot of public relations gestures as only $200 million a year is actually dedicated to the Global Fund to fight HIV/AIDS, TB [tuberculosis] and Malaria. The program has already become mired in bureaucratic and partisan red tape with its emphasis on abstinence only and pro-life stance. Similarly, the World Health Organization [WHO] has engaged in an ambitious program of providing 3 million people (living with AIDS) anti-retroviral [ARV] treatment by the end of 2005. The WHO calls this initiative the "3 by 5 plan." In collaboration with multilateral institutions; governments and individuals such as the World Bank, The Global Fund to Fight AIDS, Tuberculosis and Malaria; President [George W.] Bush's $15 billion pledge; the Bill and Melinda Gates Foundation, as well as other Nongovernmental Organizations, the WHO hopes to reverse Africa's HIV/AIDS epidemic.

Former President Bill Clinton has brokered a landmark AIDS deal aimed at making ARVs available to poorer countries. He hopes to make life saving drugs available to 2 million people by the year 2008. Through his efforts, countries such as Canada, Ireland, and Great Britain among others have contributed to the initiative. Ireland has already committed $58 million to Mozambique while Britain hopes to donate 320 million pounds by the year 2006. Furthermore, Britain plans to place the HIV/AIDS epidemic at the center of the G-8 [group of eight wealthiest nations] and European Union agenda in 2005. These are the types of initiatives needed in order to begin reversing the HIV/AIDS trend in sub-Saharan Africa. In addition to the aforementioned involvement at the international level, nations in the region that are severely afflicted by the pandemic, must show commitment by ensuring coordination of these HIV/AIDS programs with particular emphasis on women. The need for afflicted nations in the region to vigorously engage in public health education as well as voluntary testing, now assumes additional urgency as international initiatives targeted at the region increase. This would help to identify and target those individuals at risk for early intervention.

"Abysmal governments and spooky despots: just two of the many reasons why HIV can rage almost unchecked south of the Sahara."

Political Ignorance Contributes to the Spread of AIDS in Africa

Marco Evers

In the following viewpoint, Marco Evers reports that the fight against AIDS in sub-Saharan Africa must overcome not only social and economic constraints but also government misinformation. Citing the claims of various African leaders, Evers states that presidents and government health officials are touting cures for AIDS that are based on superstition and nonscientific remedies. More damaging, though, these same politicians and professionals are warning their populations to ignore antiretroviral medications that have proven effective in treating HIV and AIDS, Evers writes. Evers is the London correspondent for the German newsmagazine Der Spiegel.

Marco Evers, "Epidemic of Ignorance: The Difficult Struggle Against AIDS in Africa," Spiegel Online, June 8, 2007. Copyright © 2007 by Spiegel Online. All rights reserved. Reproduced by permission.

As you read, consider the following questions:

1. According to Evers, why do Africans afflicted with HIV or AIDS sometimes insist they are suffering only from related diseases like pneumonia instead of facing the reality of their predicament?

2. As Evers reports, how many South Africans die each day from AIDS?

3. What myth did South African vice president Jacob Zuma publically endorse as a postcoital protection against HIV transmission?

It's a story, set in the tiny, Western African country of Gambia, that would almost be funny—if it weren't so outrageous and tragic.

The country, clinging to the banks of the Gambia River as it winds toward the coast, is ruled by 41-year-old Yahya Jammeh, an autocrat who has a thing for white garb. And he aims high—he has resolved to transform his country into an African version of the rich, Asian city-state Singapore by 2020. Quite a goal for a country of 1.6 million with a low literacy rate and 75 percent of the population living off the land. But compared to Jammeh's most recent vision, reinventing Gambia as a center of trade and finance sounds almost plausible.

A Miracle Healer

Jammeh—a military officer who staged a successful putsch [attempt to overthrow the government] in 1994—is not just the president. He's also a healer on a divine mission. In January of this year [2007], he summoned a number of his acolytes together with foreign diplomats and revealed to them that he had made an extraordinary discovery. He announced that, in addition to asthma, he was now capable of healing Acquired Immune Deficiency Syndrome (AIDS)—the epidemic that ravages sub-Saharan Africa like no other region of the world. More than 15 million Africans have already died of

AIDS, and a further 25 million are infected with the HIV virus which causes the disease.

On Thursdays—Jammeh's healing powers are only available to him on that day of the week he says—the president frequently allows Gambian television to film him as he defeats AIDS: Patients lie flat on their backs as the president whirls around them and mumbles verses from the Koran. He slaps green sludge onto their skin, sprinkles liquid from an old Evian bottle over them and gives them a brown broth to drink. A quick banana snack completes the therapy.

That's it. Thanks to the power of the Koran and seven secret herbs this treatment, repeated over the course of several weeks, leads to the patient being cured of the lethal virus "with absolute certainty," as Jammeh says. But two requirements need to be met for it all to work. First: His patients have to renounce alcohol, tea, coffee and sex for the duration of their treatment—as well as theft. And second: Whoever is taking anti-viral medication has to stop doing so immediately, according to Jammeh.

Even more disturbing is that the Gambian minister of health supports his president—despite being a trained gynecologist educated in Ukraine and Ireland. The country's other institutions, including the parliament, are doing the same. And on the streets of Gambia, demonstrations can sometimes be seen—not against Jammeh, but in support of him.

"Curing" AIDS with Herbs and Bananas

So far, one of the few within Gambia to voice any criticism has been the United Nations spokesperson there, Fadzai Gwaradzimba. She said there was no proof for the success of Jammeh's method and that no one should believe they would no longer be infected following treatment by the president. Jammeh was so enraged that he immediately declared the UN representative unwelcome and forced her to leave the country within 48 hours.

Earlier, two high-ranking AIDS educators had already announced their resignation in the capital city of Banjul. They explained that, in light of Jammeh's healing mania, it was impossible to teach the population about the dangers of HIV and AIDS. Meanwhile Jammeh continues to up the ante. In early April he announced he has now acquired the ability to heal diabetes, and that—just as with asthma—he needs only five minutes to do so. Not all his subjects believe him—but quite a few do.

Abysmal governments and spooky despots: just two of the many reasons why HIV can rage almost unchecked south of the Sahara. Only a handful of African states have adopted a rational approach to AIDS. Senegal, Ghana and especially Uganda have achieved impressive results in their struggle against the spread of the virus. But in other African societies conditions often prevail that actually help HIV spread—even now, 25 years after the discovery of the lethal disease.

Everything is connected: superstition, illiteracy, poverty, disinformation, isolation, corruption, migration, prostitution, promiscuity, polygamy—and, of course, the silence. Even though AIDS represents a grade-A catastrophe in many parts of sub-Saharan Africa, the issue has remained taboo. No one speaks about it, no one confesses to being affected by it—neither those infected nor their relatives, neither religious leaders nor politicians.

Those who know they are infected prefer to claim they're not suffering from AIDS but only from the plethora of diseases that take hold thanks to the weakening of the immune system—tumors, for example, tuberculosis or pneumonia. Some even claim to have been bewitched. Everything is better than AIDS, since AIDS is still considered the disease of shame.

The eldest son of former South African President Nelson Mandela died of the effects of AIDS at age 54, in early 2005. His father made the affliction public and urged his compatriots to finally speak openly about the epidemic—to no avail. In many parts of Africa, those who admit to being HIV-positive must fear being ostracized along with their relatives. Some have even been killed by angry neighbors after making their HIV-positive status public.

Disinformation, Corruption, and Silence

It's bizarre how so many countries succeed in denying an epidemic that sends masses of young people to the grave and hollows out entire societies from within. Farmers afflicted with AIDS are too weak to work in the fields. Teachers no longer teach. Soldiers die. Truck drivers, engineers, doctors and ministers, their wives and their children—they are all affected. AIDS is costing many countries all the economic progress made during the last 25 years.

Some companies routinely hire two applicants for a job opening because they know very well that soon only one of them will be left. Burials have become the most frequent family occasions in many regions. Twenty-five years ago, life expectancy in Botswana was still above 60. Now it has sunk to little more than 40. Twelve-million children have become orphans due to AIDS. Many of them were infected with the virus before they were born or from their mother's milk.

Hardly any of these countries has even a semi-functional health system. Scientifically trained medical practitioners are rare and most of the ill seldom come into contact with them, if at all. Doctors can only estimate the overall infection rate, for example, by means of testing those they do come into contact with—pregnant women for example. And what they've found is breathtaking even for pessimistic experts. Every fifth person in Zambia, every fourth person in Namibia and every third birth in Zimbabwe and Botswana is HIV positive. With the exception of India, the absolute number of people with HIV is nowhere higher than in South Africa. The figure is above 6 million. More than a thousand South Africans die of AIDS every day.

Estimated Lives Lost in South Africa Due to AIDS Denial and the Resulting Failure to Distribute Antiretrovirals (ARVs)

Year	Adult HIV Prevalence (%)	No. AIDS Deaths	Pts. on ARV Treatment (%)	Pts. Who Could Have Been Treated (%)	Difference (%)	Attributable Lost Lives	ARV Life-Yrs./Pt.	Total Life-Yrs. Lost
2000	20.1	270,000	<3	5	2	5400	6.7	36,180
2001	20.1	270,000	<3	10	7	18,900	6.7	126,630
2002	18.6	290,000	<3	20	17	49,300	6.7	330,310
2003	18.6	290,000	3	30	27	78,300	6.7	524,610
2004	18.8	320,000	<10	40	30	96,000	6.7	643,200
2005	18.8	320,000	23	50	27	86,400	6.7	578,880
Total						334,300		2.2 mil.

TAKEN FROM: Pride Chigwedere et al., "Estimating the Lost Benefits of Antiretroviral Drug Use in South Africa," Journal of Acquired Immune Deficiency Syndromes, December 1, 2008.

Africans still go to their highly respected traditional healers for medical aid, healers that follow the tradition of their forefathers by tackling all ills with herbs and magic. In the best possible scenario, these healers could help solve the AIDS problem, and in many countries aid organizations are trying to recruit them for necessary educational work. But often the messages spread by such healers are part of the problem. In southern Africa, for example, millions of men are convinced an HIV infection can easily be cured—by means of sex with a virgin.

Persistent Legends Increase the Suffering

That condoms offer protection is far from common knowledge, and many of those who have heard don't believe it. Some believe condoms are irreconcilable with masculinity or even take them to be a conspiracy by white men aimed at lowering the African birth rate. Many also believe that condoms are infected with HIV by the West to reduce the African population. Many tribal leaders and traditional healers warn against the use of condoms—as does the Catholic Church. Under such circumstances, messages of prevention are often ignored.

Tragically, the HIV virus strikes people who are especially predisposed to it in Africa. Other venereal diseases such as syphilis, herpes or gonorrhea are also still widespread in the region—and they tend to make those who suffer from them more susceptible to the AIDS virus.

In addition, many women in Sub-Saharan Africa have for generations been engaging in sexual practices that dramatically increase their own risk of infection. Before having sex, they use herbs, powder or cloths to remove all moisture from their vaginas. Men supposedly appreciate this practice because it makes the vagina dry, hot and tight. But so-called "dry sex" often leads to minor injuries to the mucous membrane, which facilitates HIV infection. AIDS educators are trying to encourage women to abandon this custom, but with only limited success.

In theory, South Africa is the country that should be best equipped, in terms of economic power and infrastructure, to fight the epidemic. But South African politicians seem to be doing all they can to help the virus spread. They may not be quite as flamboyant as Gambia's presidential virus slayer, but they come close to being as dangerous. Thabo Mbeki, Mandela's successor as president, has repeatedly flirted with the long discredited ideas of the "AIDS dissidents," according to whom, AIDS is not caused by a virus, but by poverty and malnutrition.

Ignorance Even of Officials

Mbeki's former vice president, Jacob Zuma, has had unprotected sex with a woman who was HIV positive at the time. There was hardly any risk of infection, Zuma said publicly, since he showered immediately after having sex. It's astonishing that Zuma isn't more knowledgeable about the spread of HIV; he was, after all, previously the director of a national AIDS organization.

And the South African minister of health, a med-school graduate, advises those infected not to take anti-viral medication in favor of a mixture of garlic, lemon, potatoes and red beet. That's better, she says, because the side effects are less severe. "Dr. Red Beet," as she is mockingly called, also sympathizes with German miracle healer Matthias Rath, who sells vitamin drinks in South Africa as an alleged alternative to established HIV medication.

In wealthier nations, AIDS has long ceased leading inevitably to death. The disease may not be curable, but modern medication can battle the viruses so effectively that it can no longer be detected in the blood. For a long time, however, the therapy was so expensive that only some 100,000 Africans benefited from it in 2003.

But things have changed—and this is the only positive piece of news about AIDS in Africa. Many countries and organizations provide billions of dollars to purchase medication at drastically reduced prices. Last year [2006], about 1.3 million AIDS victims in sub-Saharan Africa had access to the medication they need to survive for the first time.

In other words, almost a third of those in need already receive help. By 2010, the UN wants to ensure that every afflicted person receives treatment.

The end of the epidemic could be near for African HIV patients. But the hurdles remain high: For the afflicted to be cured, their blood first needs to be examined by qualified personnel—of which there is a considerable lack. Hardly 10 percent of the population have taken an AIDS test in the most severely affected African countries.

The others often don't even know that such a thing exists.

"In eleven [African] countries, a baby born in 2010 will live, on average, barely beyond his or her thirtieth birthday."

AIDS Is Devastating Africa's Children

Lawrence O. Gostin

In the following viewpoint, Lawrence O. Gostin discusses the devastation wrought by the AIDS pandemic in sub-Saharan Africa, particularly among women and children. Mother-to-infant transmission, which has been dramatically reduced in North America and Europe using antiretroviral medication, is still a large problem in Africa. He notes that in sub-Saharan Africa, women transmit infection to their infants at a rate of 21 to 43 percent. Gostin calls on Africa's governments as well as international organizations to continue the fight to end the disease so that Africa's children can enjoy a healthy future. Lawrence O. Gostin is an American law professor who specalizes in public health law, as well as a prolific contributor to journals on medicine and law.

Lawrence O. Gostin, "AIDS in Africa Among Women and Infants: A Human Rights Framework," *The Hastings Center Report*, vol. 32, no. 5, September–October 2002, p. 9.

As you read, consider the following questions:

1. What is the rate of HIV infection among women attending antenatal clinics in sub-Saharan Africa, according to the author?

2. What are some barriers to reducing mother-to-infant HIV/AIDS transmission in sub-Saharan Africa, in Gostin's opinion?

3. How is access to medical care for HIV/AIDS related to human rights, according to the author?

It is difficult to overestimate the devastation of the AIDS pandemic in sub-Saharan Africa. In that region, 9 percent of all adults are HIV-infected. Africa will soon reach premature death rates not seen since the end of the nineteenth century. In eleven countries, a baby born in 2010 will live, on average, barely beyond his or her thirtieth birthday.

The rate of HIV infection among women attending antenatal clinics in sub-Saharan Africa ranges from 10 to 50 percent, with an average rate in some countries of around 30 percent. Women transmit infection to their infants in this region at a rate of 21 to 43 percent. The tragedy is that AIDS in Africa is largely preventable, with models of success found in Uganda and Senegal, where HIV incidence among pregnant women and infants has significantly declined.

Mother-to-Infant Transmission

In North America and Europe, mother-to-infant transmission has been dramatically reduced using a regimen of antiretroviral medication administered to pregnant women and newborns. The estimated cost of the regimen ($200 with discounts in pricing) makes the treatment unavailable to most people in sub-Saharan Africa where the annual health expenditure per person is between $2 and $40. Additional barriers include the difficulty of complying with a regimen that entails administering a drug four to five times daily for weeks, the limited infrastructure for distributing drugs and monitoring compliance, and inadequate maternal-child health care services.

Research in sub-Saharan Africa and Southeast Asia has shown that less expensive short-course antiretroviral regimens diminish perinatal transmission by one-third to one-half. A trial in Uganda of a single oral dose of nevirapine given to the mother and newborn had similar benefits. These results held regardless of whether women breastfed the child, although the formula-fed groups had greater reductions in transmission. Economic analyses suggest that short-course therapies can achieve significant health and financial benefits compared with the cost of the therapy. As a result, WHO [World Health Organization] and UNAIDS recommend short-course perinatal antiretroviral therapy and advise HIV-infected women not to breastfeed their infants, where this can be accomplished safely.

Despite the clinical research, economic analysis, and public health guidance, few developing countries have national policies for integrating antiretroviral therapy into antenatal clinics. Those resisting these kind of interventions object on grounds of economics and ethics, but neither argument is convincing. Thabo Mbeki, president of South Africa, has seen the HIV/AIDS pandemic as part of institutionalized racism and has resisted guaranteeing all pregnant women antiretroviral treatment; he made nevirapine available only at a number of limited pilot sites. In response to his intransigence, the Treatment Action Campaign (TAC) sued, claiming a human right to health for pregnant women and infants.

A Lawsuit to Get Treatment

Under the South African Bill of Rights, "Everyone has the right to have access to health care services, including reproductive health care" ([section] 27(1)(a)). The state must "take

AIDS Orphans Lose Out

Besides problems associated with poverty, orphaned children experience a variety of psychological problems. They are denied the basic closeness of family life, parental love, attention, and affection. As parents and other family members become ill, children take on greater responsibility for income generation, food production, and care of family members. Many of them are likely to drop out from school. A [2002] review by UNICEF [United Nations Children's Fund] on the effects of orphaning on schooling and child labor in 20 sub-Saharan African countries revealed that in all countries, children aged 15 to 24 who had lost one or both parents were less likely to be in school and more likely to be working more than 40 hours a week. . . . Sometimes due to poverty, orphans may be coerced into the sex trade, which predisposes them to HIV, and once infected it is difficult for them to access good health care. Cases of orphans being abused by foster parents, adults or guardians are not hard to find. In some cases, orphans and widows can lose property and inheritance rights, a situation that can enhance their poverty. This increases the risk of psychosocial distress that can hinder their ability to cope.

Joe L.P. Lugalla,
Journal of Developing Societies,
March 2003.

reasonable legislative and other measures, within its available resources, to achieve the progressive realisation of each of these rights." Additionally; "every child has the right to basic nutrition, shelter, basic health care serves and social services" ([section] 28(1)(c)). The Constitutional Court of South Africa has made clear that the state must afford citizens access to these socio-economic rights, although there is no self-standing, enforceable right to a minimum core level of services.

In its suit, the TAC challenged the government policy of limiting the use of nevirapine only to specific research and training sites. The Constitutional Court rejected all four reasons proffered by the government for preventing the vast majority of pregnant women from gaining access to treatment: ineffectiveness, drug resistance, safety, and capacity.

First, the Court found that nevirapine will save countless infants from contracting HIV infection perinatally, even if it is administered without full support services. For example, even though there are cultural taboos and health hazards entailed in bottle feeding (especially where women do not have access to clean water), nevirapine will reduce perinatal transmission. Second, although resistant strains of HIV might exist after a single dose of nevirapine, this mutation is likely to be transient. More importantly, the possibility of drug resistance is small in comparison with the benefits. Third, although there are adverse effects with the long-term administration of antiretrovirals, there is no evidence of harm to mother and infant by providing a single tablet of nevirapine to the mother and a few drops to her baby at the time of birth. Finally, although government lacks the infrastructure and resources to provide comprehensive HIV prevention services to women and infants (for example, testing, counseling, long-term treatment, and infant formula), it has ample capacity to provide single-dose therapy.

The Greatest Threat to Public Health

The Court made clear that its principal concerns were for indigent women who could not afford treatment and newborns who were entitled to special protection. The "rigid and inflexible" policy denying mothers and their newborn children treatment violates the state's constitutional duty to take reasonable measures, within its available resources, to achieve the progressive realization of the right to have access to health care services. "A potentially lifesaving drug was on offer and ... could have been administered within the available resources of the state without any known harm to mother or child." Further, the policy of waiting for a protracted period before taking a decision on the use of nevirapine beyond the research and training sites is also constitutionally unreasonable.

"We know," said the Court, "that throughout the country health services are overextended. HIV/AIDS is but one of many illnesses that require attention. It is, however, the greatest threat to public health in our country. 'During the last two decades, the HIV pandemic has entered our consciousness as an incomprehensible calamity. HIV/AIDS has claimed millions of lives, inflicting pain and grief, causing fear and uncertainty, and threatening the economy.'"

TAC v. Minister of Health is a bold judicial decision in a country with a history of racial apartheid, a new constitution, and devastating conditions of poverty. The Court rejected the claim that it lacks the power to compel the state to act. Rather, citing [the 1954 US desegration ruling] *Brown v. Board of Education*, the Court ruled that the "government is constitutionally bound to give effect to such orders [regarding socioeconomic rights] whether or not they affect its policy and has to find the resources to do so." Consequently, the Court ordered the government to develop a program for prevention of perinatal HIV transmission, including counseling and testing pregnant women, counseling HIV-infected pregnant women, and making appropriate treatment available. In particular, the Court ordered the government without delay to remove restrictions on access to nevirapine and facilitate its use throughout the country.

From Ethics to Life-Saving Treatment

It is difficult to believe that only a few years ago the bioethics community in North America focused on the ethics of clinical trials of short-course HIV treatment, rather than the unconscionable burden of disease among African women and children. [*New England Journal of Medicine* editor in chief] Marcia Angell harshly compared the short-course trials to the infamous Tuskegee study because of the placebo-controlled design. Yet in the short-course studies, the subjects gave informed consent and were not exposed to risk; the studies were designed to benefit host countries, which desired the research and ethically approved the protocols; and the results had the potential vastly to improve the lives of the world's poorest and disadvantaged mothers and children. The short-course studies included the Ugandan trial, which found a dramatic benefit from a single oral dose of nevirapine. And now the Constitutional Court of South Africa rules that women and infants have a human right to that drug. The decision will save the lives of countless children and, no doubt, influence governments and courts in the African continent and beyond.

> *"An expanding network of centers . . .*
> *with a unifying goal of catalyzing ex-*
> *panded access to care and treatment*
> *for HIV-infected children and their*
> *families [now exists in Africa]."*

Treatment for African Children with AIDS Is Expanding

Mark W. Kline

In the following viewpoint, from a speech he delivered to the Association of Third World Studies, Mark W. Kline describes how some generous funding and international commitment led to the creation of a pediatric AIDS clinic in Romania, a European country plagued by the disease. Kline reports that the operation, which began in 2001, was very successful at providing care and antiretroviral medications to Romania's children, significantly lowering the childhood AIDS mortality rate within three years. Kline and his colleagues repeated the project in Botswana with the same results, and the encouraging reduction in AIDS deaths led him to broaden the project to other African nations. Kline

Mark W. Kline, "AIDS in Africa: On the Cusp of Hope," *Journal of Third World Studies*, vol. 25, no. 2, 2008, pp. 11–19. Copyright © 2008 by the Association of Third World Studies, Inc. Reprinted with the permission of Association of Third World Studies Inc., P.O., Box 1232, Americus, GA 31709-1232.

insists that building these care centers in African nations has had a positive impact on the health of children and, by getting anti-retroviral drugs to those in need, improved the longevity of youngsters living with the disease. Kline is a professor of pediatrics at Baylor University College of Medicine in Houston, Texas. He also is director of the AIDS International Training and Research Program at that institution.

As you read, consider the following questions:

1. What are two of the reasons Kline gives to explain why African children do not have access to HIV and AIDS treatment?

2. As the author reports, what was the mortality rate of children living with AIDS in Romania in 2001, after the Romanian-American Children's Center opened? What was the mortality rate in 2004, after the center had been in operation for just three years?

3. According to Kline, in what African countries have he and his colleagues contributed to developing pediatric AIDS treatment centers as of 2008?

Looking at a map of the world demonstrates that there is no continent that has been spared the HIV/AIDS epidemic, but particularly hard hit have been the countries of southern Africa. There are now seven countries in southern Africa that have adult HIV prevalence rates exceeding 25 percent. That rolls off the tongue fairly easily, but when you stop to think about that it really is very sobering. More than one (1) in four (4) of the adult population is infected with HIV. Ninety-five percent of the 13,400 new HIV infections and 8500 HIV/AIDS-associated deaths that occur each day are in developing countries. This has become a disease of the developing world. What is less well appreciated is that children now account for 14 percent of all new infections and 18 percent of all deaths. Children now represent a sizable proportion of new infections and deaths. This translates to 1560 HIV/AIDS-associated deaths per day among children worldwide, the death of a child every minute of every hour, 24 hours a day, 365 days of the year. Across southern Africa today funeral homes are open 24 hours a day, seven days a week to accommodate the demand. . . .

HIV/AIDS is having a devastating impact on Africans in their most productive years. The median age of death for women in southern Africa today is 26 years. The median age of death for men is 29 years. HIV/AIDS has shaved 30 years of life expectancy, erasing decades of public health gains. For anyone who has worked on any pediatric ward in any public hospital in sub-Saharan Africa in the past decade, this is a very familiar image: a stunted, wasted HIV-infected infant or toddler dying with AIDS, often with chronic diarrheal disease or tuberculosis or some other type of respiratory infection. In 2006, UNICEF [United Nations Childrens Fund] estimated that HIV/AIDS accounted for about four percent of all child deaths globally. . . . In Botswana, for example, 57.7 percent of all child deaths now are attributed to HIV/AIDS. HIV/AIDS is becoming the dominant cause of mortality across the region for children. And deaths, of course, are only a part of the story. There is the AIDS orphan crisis. More than 15 million African children already have been orphaned by HIV/AIDS and it's estimated that by 2010 there will be 20 million AIDS orphans. These are children destined for lives of poverty, illiteracy, disease and early death.

Children Not Getting Treatment

Stephen Lewis, special envoy to Africa from the United Nations said in January of 2005, "In the instance of antiretroviral therapy, the scenario for children is quite simply doomsday." But, why should this be the case a decade after the advent of HAART [highly active antiretroviral therapy] for American and European [children] with HIV/AIDS? Why should African children still be waiting for their opportunity to take life-saving treatment? The fact is that HIV-infected children are underrepresented among those accessing treatment in virtually every setting worldwide. Across Africa, in the few places where HIV/AIDS treatment programs have been started, adults are receiving treatment almost exclusively. It's not uncommon to go to a treatment site to see that there are 2000 or more adults on treatment for HIV, but literally fewer than ten children.

The reasons for this disparity in access to treatment are varied. Currently, it is estimated that no more than 60,000 children worldwide receive antiretroviral treatment. This is fewer than three percent of all HIV-infected children globally. The treatments of which we're so proud and which have had a transformative impact on HIV-infected children in the United States have not had a meaningful impact for children in the developing world. So, what are the barriers? There has been a lack of infrastructure. The clinics for administering care and treatment have not existed. The laboratories for monitoring the treatment appropriately have not existed. There has been a lack and loss of human capacity to deliver care and treatment. The productive capacity of African schools to produce doctors, nurses, pharmacists and other health professionals is very low. There also is an exodus of professionals from the region to the developed world, the so-called African brain drain. In addition there is the death of professionals from HIV/AIDS. In Africa today, more health professionals die than retire and about 60 percent of the deaths can be attributed to HIV/AIDS.

One of the most important barriers to treatment of HIV-infected children has been a lack of commitment. This sounds very strange in some sense because most of us, I think, would probably give top priority to the treatment of children, but in fact, in a number of settings across Africa adults have been given priority. One government official said to me on one occasion that the adults were given priority because if they were treated they could produce more children to replace those that died. When a child with HIV receives treatment, that child does not go back to work, he or she does not pay taxes, and they don't vote. Finally, there is the perceived complexity of pediatric treatment. Among health professionals the feeling is that HIV-infected children are somehow too difficult to treat; that the drugs are too strong or they can't be monitored appropriately. These are all myths, but as health professionals we have to do a better job of educating our colleagues.

The AIDS Plight in Romania

The Baylor College of Medicine International Pediatric AIDS Initiative began not in Africa, but in Romania. I had been a pediatric HIV specialist for about a decade when I made a trip in early 1996 to Romania that really changed me. There is no other way to say it. I was floored by what I saw in Romania: thousands of HIV-infected children warehoused in large orphanages, sick with HIV and dying from AIDS. This was a legacy of the communist era, during which children were given transfusions of human blood and there was rampant use and reuse of disposable needles. It is estimated that about 11,000 children became infected with HIV during that time period.

Today, Romania accounts for over half of all European pediatric HIV/AIDS cases. This little country, the size of Oregon, with only about 24 million people has more than half of all of the cases of HIV/AIDS in Europe. And children account for 90 percent of all HIV/AIDS cases in Romania. Romania in fact is the only country on earth where there are more HIV-infected children than adults. As I mentioned, most of these children were infected with HIV in medical institutions through the transfusion of infected blood and the use and reuse of disposable needles. Some of these children continue to reside in institutions even still. Others now live on the streets of Bucharest, where they beg from passing motorists and pedestrians during the day, and descend into the sewers at night for warmth. Many of the children have grown into adolescence and even young adulthood.

When we started working in Romania in 1996 we gravitated to ... the Municipal Hospital in the Black Sea port of Constanta. Constanta has been hard hit by the HIV/AIDS epidemic. In fact, if you look at one of the popular travel atlases on Romania, the very first sentence of the description of Constanta says that it is the "pediatric AIDS capital of the world." That's a bit of an overstatement, but HIV/AIDS has been a serious problem in Constanta. When we began working at the Constanta Municipal Hospital, we met children like George. George was ten years old ... and weighed about forty pounds. He was the size of an average four year old. Alina was 11 years old. ... These are two of several hundred children who lived with HIV and died of AIDS in the late 1990s at the Constanta Municipal Hospital without ever having an opportunity to take an antiretroviral drug at a time when those medications were routinely available for American children. ...

Building a Pediatric Treatment Center

We began examining the children and cataloging their health problems. We treated their diarrheal disease, we gave them nutritional supplements, we treated their tuberculosis and we created a computerized database so that we could track their health outcomes. Doing these very simple things relatively inexpensively, we began to see modest improvements in their health. We worked with the nurses and doctors to educate them about HIV. ... We had seen that there was a lot of cross infection occurring in the hospital and we wanted to reduce that risk to the children's health. Again, we saw modest improvements in health. But we knew that to transform the health of HIV-infected children in Constanta we had to introduce HAART as had occurred in the United States.

To contextualize this a little bit for you, this was at the time when most experts were saying that the kinds of therapies we were using for HIV-infected children in the U.S. would never be practical or affordable in a developing world setting. They were saying that it couldn't be done.

Beginning in about 1999, we began talking with some of our Romanian colleagues about the possibility of building a pediatric HIV treatment center. The Constanta Municipal Hospital, subsequently renamed the Infectious Diseases Hospital Constanta, donated an old abandoned orphanage and became our partner in the project. Now, we had a little problem, and that was that when we put the plans together and the estimate was that it would cost about $500,000 to rehabilitate the building and open it as a pediatric HIV/AIDS center. Just at that time the *Houston Chronicle* published a large feature story on pediatric AIDS that was titled "Worlds Apart," and it contrasted the advances that had been made in the care and treatment of HIV-infected children in the United States with what was happening in the developing world. The medical writer, Leigh Hopper, and the photographer, Smiley Pool, had traveled with my team to Romania. In the article they mentioned that we had a dream of building a pediatric HIV/AIDS center in Romania. This was a 26-page feature story, the largest the *Houston Chronicle* had ever done.

The very next day I was sitting in my office when I received a call from a woman named Sister Olive. I picked up the phone and this lady said, "My name is Sister Olive, I'm the CEO of the Sisters of Charity of the Incarnate Word. You know, we were having our annual board of directors meeting in Houston over the weekend and on Saturday we spent a lot of time talking about our mission statement. The Pope has declared a jubilee year and he's asked all of the congregations to look over their mission statements to see if they should be changed or expanded in some way. On Saturday we discussed pediatric AIDS as a possible expansion of our mission. Then, the Sunday newspaper arrived and we saw this incredible story about your program. It says in that story that you want to build a clinic for HIV-infected children in Romania. How much is that going to cost?" I told her that it would cost about half a million dollars. She said, "If I send you a check for $300,000, will it help?" I said, "Yes, it would help quite a lot." This is not the kind of call I get everyday, but on Friday of that week I received a check in the mail for $300,000. And with the help of the Sisters of Charity and the Abbott Fund we took this old building and rehabilitated it and nine months later opened it as the Romanian-American Children's Center.

Transforming Lives in Romania

In partnership with our colleagues at the Infectious Diseases Hospital Constanta, the Romanian-American Children's Center has transformed the care and treatment of HIV-infected children. There is a large outpatient clinic on the ground floor and on the second floor there are classrooms for the education and training of health professionals from across the region. Every known HIV-infected child and adolescent in Constanta County is in care in this Center, which today is the biggest pediatric HIV treatment center in Europe. Record numbers of children with HIV have been permitted back into the public schools. The wasted and stunted HIV-infected children that I met in the mid-1990s now have grown very tall and look perfectly healthy.

We have collected reams of data to show the benefits that have accrued to children who are treated for HIV in Constanta, but I'm going to [mention just one statistic]. This is the annual death rate for HIV-infected children in care at the Romanian-American Children's Center, which we have tracked very carefully beginning in 1998 through the present.... In the four-year period 1998–2001, an average of 13 percent of all of the known HIV-infected children died each year. The Center opened in April of 2001 and we started the program of

HAART in the Center in November of 2001. . . . The death rate . . . dropped to seven percent, then three percent, and then to less than one percent in 2004. This is the difference between 109 child deaths in 2001 and seven deaths in 2004. This was really a remarkable outcome. It was an amazing thing to be part of and something we wanted to replicate.

Repeating the Process in Africa

Africa is obviously where we needed to replicate it. At the time, Africa's worst epidemic was in Botswana. President [Festus] Mogae of Botswana had said, "We are threatened with extinction." At the time I think a lot of people thought this was a bit of exaggeration, but what society can afford to lose 25 or 30 percent of its most productive members and remain viable? We had begun working in Botswana in 1999 and had an excellent relationship there with the Minister of Health, Ms. Joy Phumaphi. I said to her, "Look, this is what has happened in Romania, we built the clinic, we started a program of treatment, here's the short term impact it has had. Would you be willing to partner on the creation of a similar facility in Botswana?" She said that they would and asked what I needed from the government. I said, "I need a piece of land. If you'll give me a piece of land, I'll go out and look for funding to put up the building and run the program." . . .

The Ministry of Health provided land directly across the breezeway from the pediatric ward [of the Princess Marina Hospital] for a pediatric HIV center. The Bristol-Myers Squibb Foundation provided a grant to build and operate the Center for five years. Because we didn't want children dying of AIDS while we were putting up a building, we renovated two little store rooms at the Princess Marina Hospital. We slapped a sign on the wall that said "Bana Clinic." "Bana" is the Setswana word for child. We began canvassing the pediatric ward and talking to the parents and telling them that if they wanted their children tested for HIV to bring them to the Bana Clinic, and that if they had been tested for HIV and were positive to bring them to the Bana Clinic because we had antiretroviral medications available. We began to treat children for HIV/AIDS. These were the first children in Botswana ever to get treatment for HIV. By the time our main clinic was built and open, we had more than 200 children on treatment in the Bana Clinic. . . . It's called the Baylor-Botswana Children's Clinical Center of Excellence. This Center has had an enormous impact on pediatric HIV/AIDS in Botswana, as the Center in Constanta had on pediatric HIV/AIDS. . . .

We're not talking about an additional six months or twelve months or eighteen months of life expectancy, but rather about children who would be dead at two or three or four years of age who can expect to live to 30 or 40 or so years of age. It's literally the difference between living and dying.

Reversing Childhood AIDS Deaths

The death rate for pediatric HIV/AIDS in Botswana has plummeted just as the death rate in Romania plummeted. The Center opened in 2003 and . . . the death rate has declined. In 2006, we recorded a death rate of 0.3 percent, just five deaths out of nearly 2000 children in care in the Center. I'm sure this is not the image you have in your heads of what pediatric AIDS in Africa is. The children are living instead of dying. By the way, this is the lowest pediatric HIV/AIDS death rate ever recorded for any large pediatric center anywhere in the world, not just in Africa, but western Europe or the United States or anywhere else. African children can benefit from therapy just as children in the U.S. and Western Europe have.

This experience caused a lot of people to rethink their positions concerning the treatment of HIV-infected children in Africa. It obviously was clear evidence that children could be treated with direct benefit. In January of 2004 we announced that we wanted to replicate the Botswana experience by creating a network of children's centers across Africa and around the world to catalyze expanded access to treatment for HIV-infected children. This network has grown dramatically over the past three years. . . . We now have built and opened children's centers in Mbabane, Swaziland and Maseru, Lesotho, two small African countries hard hit by HIV/AIDS, as well as in Lilongwe, Malawi and Kampala, Uganda, where we now have more than 4000 children on treatment. We have additional centers under devlopment in Bobo Dioulasso, Burkina Faso and Kisumu, Kenya. So, this is an expanding network of centers all cooperating with one another, exchanging best clinical practices, exchanging trainees, really with a unifying goal of catalyzing expanded access to care and treatment for HIV-infected children and their families. . . .

All of these centers are collaborative. They are built and operated under collaborative agreements between Baylor College of Medicine, Texas Children's Hospital and the host governments. The government is always our primary partner. We don't want to compete with government, we don't want to duplicate anything government is doing. We want to be integrated into existing public health systems. The centers are comprehensive. They're HIV/AIDS focused, but we provide primary care to the children and we also provide care to their HIV-infected family members. So, the mother or father or both, as well as other HIV-infected family members all can get care and treatment from the centers. The centers are care and treatment, rather than research, focused. I often say that African children are not dying for lack of access to research; they are dying from lack of access to care and treatment. And the centers are really designed to provide support for regional and national scale-up of pediatric and family HIV/AIDS care and treatment. They serve the communities in which they are located, but they should be impacting much broader geographic regions. In addition to the direct benefits, there are a number of spinoff benefits of these centers. They're building capacity for pediatric healthcare and clinical research generally. As we elevate the level of care for HIV-infected children, we should also be enhancing the care of children with other life-threatening diseases. I call these collateral benefits. You may have heard the term "collateral damage" with respect to HIV/AIDS. In public health circles people talk about collateral damage. They say that as resources are diverted away from vaccine preventable diseases, diarrheal disease, respiratory disease, and so forth, into HIV/AIDS, mortality rates from those other causes will start to rise. But here we have an opportunity really to produce benefit for children with a variety of life-threatening conditions. We also think we can do something to reverse brain drain by attracting African health professionals back to Africa by giving them appropriate work environments and appropriate tools to do their work. The centers are a powerful impetus for HIV testing and they also have a powerful destigmatizing effect.

Periodical Bibliography

The following articles have been selected to supplement the diverse views presented in this chapter.

Amusa Saheed Balogun — "Islamic Perspectives on HIV/AIDS and Antiretroviral Treatment: The Case of Nigeria," *African Journal of AIDS Research*, vol. 9, no. 4, 2010.

Begna F. Dugassa — "Women's Rights and Women's Health During HIV/AIDS Epidemics: The Experience of Women in Sub-Saharan Africa," *Health Care for Women International*, August 2009.

Glenda E. Gray — "Adolescent HIV—Cause for Concern in Southern Africa," *PLoS Medicine*, February 2010.

David Himmelgreen and Nancy Romero-Daza — "Bytes of Note," *Environment*, July/August 2010.

Zaryab Iqbal and Christopher Zorn — "Violent Conflict and the Spread of HIV/AIDS in Africa," *Journal of Politics*, January 2010.

Colin McInnes — "HIV, AIDS and Conflict in Africa: Why Isn't It (Even) Worse?," *Review of International Studies*, February 1, 2011.

Fraser G. McNeill — "'Condoms Cause AIDS': Poison, Prevention and Denial in Venda, South Africa," *African Affairs*, July 2009.

Brooke G. Schoepf — "Assessing AIDS Research in Africa: Twenty-Five Years Later," *African Studies Review*, April 2010.

Clare Wilson — "How to Eradicate AIDS," *New Scientist*, February 21, 2009.

Jeremy Youde — "Government AIDS Policies and Public Opinion in Africa," *Politikon: South African Journal of Political Studies*, August 2009.

OPPOSING
VIEWPOINTS®
SERIES

CHAPTER 4

What US Policies Will Best Serve Africa?

Chapter Preface

In December 2010, the people of Tunisia took to the streets in several cities to demonstrate against high food prices, unemployment, and government corruption. After police and government security forces struck back in early January 2011, causing some casualties among the protesters, the demonstrations grew. That month, facing increasing pressure and failing support among his ministers and the military, the country's president, Zine El Abidine Ben Ali, fled. The Tunisian army restored order, and a new government was formed from various political parties within the country.

In response to the Tunisian uprising, US president Barack Obama voiced his support in a statement given on January 14. "I applaud the courage and dignity of the Tunisian people," Obama asserted. "The United States stands with the entire international community in bearing witness to this brave and determined struggle for the universal rights that we must all uphold, and we will long remember the images of the Tunisian people seeking to make their voices heard." Recognizing that the revolution had brewed throughout Ben Ali's twenty-three-year reign, Obama added, "Each nation gives life to the principle of democracy in its own way, grounded in the traditions of its own people, and those countries that respect the universal rights of their people are stronger and more successful than those that do not."

Writing in the *Progressive* five days after President Obama's remarks, Amitabh Pal questioned the legacy of US-Tunisian relations. Pal argued, "The United States ... backed Ben Ali during his twenty-three-year-long dictatorship, loving him for his pro-West and free-market policies. The Obama Administration changed its tune only at the last minute when things were beyond repair for the tyrant." Pal maintains that the revolution was entirely a populist movement that did not seek

US support because it did not expect any. Indeed, the United States had only to watch the events unfold without bringing any influence to bear.

The same has not been true for the role of the United States in the struggle for regime change in Tunisia's eastern neighbor, Libya. When demonstrators began planned acts of civil disobedience in mid-February 2011, Libya's leader Muammar Gadhafi swiftly retaliated. He ordered his still-loyal military to crush the revolt, and weeks of fighting ensued. Acting in concert with the United Nations, the United States called upon Gadhafi to end the attacks against his own people. After the Libyan president ignored his own cease-fire guarantee on March 18, US and British warships fired Tomahawk missiles into key command and control targets on Libyan soil, and they set up a "no fly" zone around rebel-held areas. Enraged by the foreign intrusion, Gadhafi pledged to fight "a long, drawn-out war with no limits."

President Obama vowed that America's role would be minimal in the efforts to keep Gadhafi's forces in check, but critics feared that such limited action would end up dragging the nation into war. Some suggested that the president could not leave America's role in this action so open-ended. For example, Speaker of the House of Representatives John Boehner (R-OH) issued a statement on March 20 that read, "Before any further military commitments are made, the administration must do a better job of communicating to the American people and to Congress about our mission in Libya and how it will be achieved."

This instance of military action is only one way in which the United States is engaged with the nations of Africa and the continent as a whole. In the following chapter, several politicians, journalists, and other experts examine the various roles America plays in Africa and whether these engagements are mutually beneficial.

> "We must help countries build [pro-
> democracy] institutions ... and we
> must be willing to speak out against
> erosions of democratic rights and free-
> doms—and not only once a country
> reaches a crisis point such as a coup."

The United States Should Promote Democracy in Africa

Russ Feingold

In the following viewpoint, Russ Feingold argues that the United States has a vested interest in promoting democracy in Africa. Democracy, according to Feingold, is important for keeping peace and ensuring civil rights in developing African nations. Feingold worries, though, that some African countries are backsliding as their governments harass opposition movements and keep a tight rein on the media. He believes America should take an active role in supporting fair elections in African nations and send a clear message to dictators that their attempts to subvert democracy will not be condoned. Feingold represented Wisconsin in the US Senate from 1993 to 2011, and chaired the Subcommittee on African Affairs.

Russ Feingold, "Speech to US Senate on Democracy in Africa," *Congressional Record*, March 2, 2010.

As you read, consider the following questions:

1. According to Feingold, Sudan's 2010 election was notable because it was the first multiparty election the nation had held in how many years?

2. What kinds of laws does the author claim Ethiopia has passed in recent years that threaten democracy in that country?

3. As Feingold states, what African government is supposedly using its National Intelligence Service to undermine opposition?

I would like to note the many challenges to democracy we are seeing across Africa today. I have long said that promoting and supporting democratic institutions should be a key tenet of our engagement with Africa, as good governance is essential to Africa's stability and its prosperity. Africans are well aware of this, and that is why we have seen spirited democratic movements throughout the continent, even against great odds. It is also why African leaders have committed at the African Union with the Declaration on Democracy, Political, Economic and Corporate Governance [of 2002] that they will work to enforce "the right to participate in free, credible and democratic political processes."

The previous administration [of George W. Bush] spoke often about its commitment to promote democracy in Africa and throughout the world. The current administration, too, has committed to encourage strong and sustainable democratic governments, though it has rightly acknowledged that democracy is about more than holding elections. In his speech in Ghana [in July 2009], President [Barack] Obama said:

America will not seek to impose any system of government on any nation—the essential truth of democracy is that each nation determines its own destiny. What we will do is increase assistance for responsible individuals and institutions, with a focus on supporting good governance—on parliaments, which check abuses of power and ensure that opposition voices are heard; on the rule of law, which ensures the equal administration of justice; on civic participation, so that young people get involved . . .

Sustaining Democracy Promotion

I agree that we must take a more holistic approach in our efforts to promote and support democracy. Democracy is not just about a single event every few years; it is also about an ongoing process of governance that is accountable and responsive to the needs and will of citizens. And it is about citizens having the space, encouragement, and ability to educate themselves, mobilize, and participate in that process. We must help countries build such institutions and encourage such space, and we must be willing to speak out against erosions of democratic rights and freedoms—and not only once a country reaches a crisis point such as a coup.

While some African countries have made great democratic strides, I am concerned about the fragile state of democracy on the continent, especially within a number of countries set to hold elections over the next 15 months. In particular, I am concerned by the democratic backsliding in several countries that are close U.S. partners and influential regional actors. It is notable that the Director of National Intelligence included a section on "stalled democratization" in Africa in his public testimony last month [February 2010] to the Senate Intelligence Committee on annual threat assessments. He stated:

> The number of African states holding elections continues to grow although few have yet to develop strong, enduring democratic institutions and traditions. In many cases the 'winner-take-all' ethos predominates and risks exacerbating ethnic, regional, and political divisions.

Elections are only one component of the democratic process, but still they are a significant one. The pre- and post-elections periods in many countries are ones in which democratic space and institutions are most clearly tested and face the greatest strains. They can be the periods in which democracy is at its best, but they can also be the periods in which democracy faces some of its greatest threats. This is the case not only in Africa; this is the case here in the United States, and that is why I have worked tirelessly to limit the power of wealthy interests to unduly influence our elections.

Watching African Elections Closely

Among those African countries scheduled to hold national elections in 2010 are Ethiopia, Sudan, Togo, Central African Republic, Burundi, Rwanda, Tanzania, and Burkina Faso. Guinea, Madagascar, and Niger, three countries that have recently had coups, have also committed to hold elections this year. And in early 2011, Benin, Djibouti, Uganda, Nigeria, and Chad are all scheduled to hold elections.

Of all these elections, Sudan's is already receiving significant attention, and for good reason. That election—the country's first multiparty one in 24 years—has the potential to be a historic step toward political transformation in Sudan if it is credible. However, restrictions on opposition parties and the continued insecurity in Darfur have many doubting whether the conditions even exist for credible elections. Furthermore, increasing violence within southern Sudan is very worrying. In any case, the results of Sudan's election in April will have a great influence on political dynamics within the country and region for years to come and will pave the way for southern Sudan's vote on self-determination, set for January 2011. The international community is rightly keeping a close eye on these elections, and we need to continue supporting efforts to make them credible and be prepared to speak out against any abuses or rigging.

Similarly, we need to keep a close eye on the other African countries holding important elections this year. Let me high-

Supporting Institutions That Check Consolidations of Power in African Regimes

Future progress towards democratization in Africa is dependent on strengthening of viable institutions of countervailing power, and U.S. programs to promote democracy must place greater emphasis on this task. This would include but not be limited to programs that strengthen electoral systems (as contrasted to individual elections), national legislatures, the judiciary, local government, civil society, and the press. The good news is that these are all areas in which the United States has mounted successful programs in the past. But institution building and the programs to support it take time—usually periods of 10 to 15 years, sometimes longer. Strengthening institutions also requires more nuanced programming tailored to country conditions, and especially the commitment of appropriate personnel on the ground.

Joel D. Barkan, "Advancing Democratization in Africa," Prepublication draft for a proposed Center for Strategic and International Studies Africa Program report, January 2009.

light four countries whose upcoming elections I believe also merit close attention and specific international engagement.

Backsliding in Ethiopia

The first is Ethiopia, which is set to hold elections in May. In his testimony, the Director of National Intelligence stated:

In Ethiopia, Prime Minister Meles [Zenawi] and his party appear intent on preventing a repeat of the relatively open 2005 election which produced a strong opposition showing.

Indeed, in Ethiopia, democratic space has been diminishing steadily since 2005. Over the last 2 years, the Ethiopian Parliament has passed several new laws granting broad discretionary powers to the government to arrest opponents. One such law, the Charities and Societies Proclamation, imposes direct government controls over civil society and bars any civil society group from receiving more than 10 percent of its funding from international sources to do work related to human rights, gender equality, the rights of the disabled, children's rights, or conflict resolution. Another law, the Anti-terrorism Proclamation, defines terrorism-related crimes so broadly that they could extend to nonviolent forms of political dissent and protest.

Ethiopia is an important partner of the United States and we share many interests. We currently provide hundreds of millions of dollars in aid annually to Ethiopia. That is why I have been so concerned and outspoken about these repressive measures, and that is why I believe we have a stake in ensuring that Ethiopia's democratic process moves forward, not backward. With the elections just 3 months away, several key opposition leaders remain imprisoned, most notably Birtukan Mideksa, the head of the Unity for Democracy and Justice Party. There is no way that elections can be fair, let alone credible, with opposition leaders in jail or unable to campaign freely. At the bare minimum, the international community should push for the release of these political prisoners ahead of the elections. If nothing changes, we should not be afraid to stand with the Ethiopian people and state clearly that an election in name only is an affront to their country's democratic aspirations.

Stifling Opposition in Burundi

The second country I want to highlight is Burundi. As many people will recall, Burundi was devastated by political violence throughout the 1990s, leaving over 100,000 people dead. Yet the country has made tremendous strides in recent years to recover and rebuild from its civil war. In 2005, it held multi-party national and local elections, a major milestone on its transition to peace. Burundians are set to head to the polls again this year. If these elections are fair, free, and peaceful, they have the potential to be another milestone along the path toward reconciliation, lasting stability, and democratic institutions. This would be good not only for Burundi but also for the whole of Central Africa. Burundians deserve international support and encouragement as they strive for that goal.

Still, many challenges remain. The tensions that fed and were fueled by Burundi's civil war have not entirely gone away. And there is some evidence that the parties continue to use the tools of war to pursue their political goals. According to a report by the International Crisis Group last month, "opposition parties are facing harassment and intimidation from police and the ruling party's youth wing and appear to be choosing to respond to violence with violence." Furthermore, there continue to be reports that the National Intelligence Service is being used by the ruling party to destabilize the opposition. If these trends continue, they could taint Burundi's elections and set back its peace process. The international community, which has played a big role in Burundi's peace process, cannot wait until a month before the election to speak out and engage the parties in these issues. We need to do it now.

Repressing Rights in Rwanda and Uganda

Burundi's neighbor to the north, Rwanda, is also slated to hold important elections this summer. Rwanda is another country that has come a long way. Since the genocide in 1994, the government and people of Rwanda have made impressive accomplishments in rebuilding the country and improving basic services. It is notable that Rwanda was the top reformer worldwide in the 2010 World Bank's "Doing Business Report."

President [Paul] Kagame has shown commendable and creative leadership in this respect. On the democratic front, however, Rwanda still has a long way to go.

Understandably there are real challenges to fostering democracy some 15 years after the genocide, but it is troubling that there is not more space within Rwanda for criticism and opposition voices. The State Department's 2008 Human Rights Report for Rwanda stated, "There continued to be limits on freedom of speech and of association, and restrictions on the press increased." With elections looming, there are now some reports that opposition party members in Rwanda are facing increasing threats and harassment. The international community should not shy away from pushing for greater democratic space in Rwanda, which is critical for the country's lasting stability. We fail to be true friends to the Rwandan people if we do not stand with them in the fight against renewed abuse of civil and political rights. In the next few months in the runup to the elections, it is a key time for international donors to raise these issues with [the government in the capital of] Kigali.

Finally, I would like to talk about Uganda, which is set to hold elections in February 2011. Uganda, like Rwanda, is a close friend of the United States, and we have worked together on many joint initiatives over recent years. President [Yoweri] Museveni deserves credit for his leadership on many issues both within the country and the wider region. However, at the same time, Museveni's legacy has been tainted by his failure to allow democracy to take hold in Uganda. Uganda's most recent elections have been hurt by reports of fraud, intimidation, and politically motivated prosecutions of opposition candidates. The Director of National Intelligence stated in his testimony that Uganda remains essentially a "one-party state" and said the government "is not undertaking democratic reforms in advance of the elections scheduled for 2011."

Uganda's elections next year could be a defining moment for the country and will have ramifications for the country's long-term stability. The riots in Buganda last September [2009] showed that regional and ethnic tensions remain strong in many parts of the country. Therefore, it is important that the United States and other friends of Uganda work with that country's leaders to ensure critical electoral reforms are enacted. In the consolidated appropriations act that passed in December [2009], Congress provided significant assistance for Uganda but also specifically directed the Secretary of State "to closely monitor preparations for the 2011 elections in Uganda and to actively promote . . . the independence of the election commission; the need for an accurate and verifiable voter registry; the announcement and posting of results at the polling stations; the freedom of movement and assembly and a process free of intimidation; freedom of the media; and the security and protection of candidates." . . .

Active US Involvement Is Needed Now

These challenges are not unique to Africa. Here in the United States, we too have to work constantly to ensure the integrity of our elections and our democratic processes. But I believe these upcoming elections in a number of African states could have major ramifications for the overall trajectory of democracy on the continent as well as for issues of regional security. I also believe several of these elections could significantly impact U.S. policy and strategic partnerships on the continent. For that reason, I do not believe we can wait until weeks or days before these elections to start focusing on them. We need to start engaging well in advance and helping to pave the way for truly democratic institutions and the consolidation of democracy. This includes aligning with democratic actors that speak out against repressive measures that erode political and civil rights. The Obama administration has done this well in some cases, but we need to do it more consistently and effectively. In the coming months, I hope to work with the administration to ensure we have a clear policy and the resources to that end.

> *"It would be better to jettison the entire democracy-and-human-rights baggage and simply say forthrightly that we, as a nation, support liberty and we wish liberals everywhere a good fight and godspeed."*

The United States Should Stop Promoting Democracy in Africa

Roger Kaplan

In the following viewpoint, Roger Kaplan contends that decades of democracy promotion in Africa have achieved little. Instead, according to Kaplan, the US government often has backed rulers feigning adherence to democratization while effectively denying civil rights and oppressing dissidents. In Kaplan's view, this approach only confuses African populations yearning for reform and ultimately earns their enmity. Kaplan argues that the United States should abandon its inept democracy promotion mission and allow Africans to choose their own path. Kaplan is a writer based in Washington, DC.

As you read, consider the following questions:

1. What was Zine Ben Ali's doctrine of "le changement," as Kaplan describes it?

2. According to the author, when is it appropriate for the United States to promote freedom in foreign countries?

3. In Kaplan's opinion, why are the African nations increasingly turning to China for assistance instead of to the United States?

In a peculiar way, the fall of Zine Ben Ali [in 2011], sole master of Tunisia for a quarter century, exposes the bankruptcy of a centerpiece of America's foreign policy, namely, our declared support for democracy.

Two inspiring victories for liberty this month [January 2011], in Sudan and Tunisia, were achieved with no help from America's multi-million dollar democracy industry; one might say despite it. In other countries, ranging from Algeria to Zimbabwe, passing by the Ivory Coast and Africa's longest-lasting unresolved colonial conflict, Western Sahara, the contribution of our "democracists" to freedom's cause has been zilch.

The regime of Omar el Bashir's Congress Party, based on Arab Muslim tribes from the Nile valley to the east and north of Khartoum, has been scolded by successive U.S. administrations for its violent repression of the southern Sudanese, who predominantly belong to sub-Saharan tribes that were evangelized by British missionaries a century ago. Bashir himself is under indictment by the International Tribunal for crimes committed against Muslim groups in Darfur, in Sudan's northwest.

In Tunisia, the regime of Zine Ben Ali, has for 23 years received American support as a partner for progress and more recently against terrorism.

The United States Backs Dictators

It would be quite respectable to say—it was first said by John Adams—that there is very little we can do in these remote and little-understood countries, each of which has its own discrete historical complexity. To proclaim our commitment to freedom, however, spend a lot of money saying so, and then watch like morons as freedom movements go right by us, is at the least embarrassing; at the worst, it fuels anti-Americanism and gives openings to our enemies, who as it happens are usually also enemies of freedom.

When Zine Ben Ali pushed aside the founder of modern independent Tunisia, Habib Bourguiba, in a 1987 palace coup, the cover story was that he was an efficient technocrat who would maintain the course on which the aging and ailing Bourguiba had set the country. Intent on proving Islam and modernity were not incompatible, Bourguiba promoted equal rights for women and encouraged them to enter the work force, tolerated political competition and press freedom, up to a point.

Ben Ali, citing an Islamist threat which he crushed, laid down a new social compact in the early '90s: Tunisians can do whatever they want in pursuit of commercial and entrepreneurial opportunities, but in the political realm, they can shut up and get used to it. It was called "*le Changement*" and it was the classical Carthaginian despotism in late 20th century dress. Purely formal opposition candidates stood in pro-forma elections, until Ben Ali removed all pretense and had the constitution changed to allow him to stay in office forever. No press, no labor unions, no independent civic life, which among other things meant that the liberal advances made during the Bourguiba years, notably where women are concerned, were turned back. The regime added protection to its other rackets, centralizing ordinary Mediterranean baksheesh [bribery] in the Ben Ali clan.

There is no case, at least not a strong case, for Zine Ben Ali being "our guy," in the way Congo big man Mobutu Sese Soko was in his day or the way Rwanda strong man Paul Kagame was said to be by President [Bill] Clinton. I don't think you could even say that Ben Ali was France's guy, even though French foreign policy, through socialist and conservative governments, coddled him much more overtly that we ever did. Practically the day before Ben Ali and his family fled Tunis for Jennah (a resort town in Saudi Arabia, which is full of "our guys" if the way we deal with them is any indication), [French] President [Nicolas] Sarkozy's foreign minister, Michele Aliot-Marie, was saying in the French National Assembly that perhaps Ben Ali should "sub-contract" crowd control to France. It was an astonishing thing to hear from a foreign minister and, no doubt, there will be contradictory accounts of what she meant.

While neither we nor the French can be held responsible for every [Nicaraguan dictator Anastacio] Somoza on the planet, it is a fact that neither we nor they did anything to keep Ben Ali from staying in power as long as he did. And for all the money USAID, the National Endowment for Democracy (NED), their French and German and Scandinavian equivalents, and what-all, spend on "democracy promotion," "rule of law," "human rights" and the rest, you would be hard put to find a Tunisian Martin Luther King who got any help from the American government. At the very most, we may have discreetly mentioned to Ben Ali that killing this one or keeping that one in jail without trial (or even charges) is not a terribly good idea, and the quiet word may even have saved a life.

US Democracy Promotion Achieves Little

The reason this matters is that it shows how bankrupt our democracy-promotion programs are. You can argue that the U.S. should not be in the democracy business, as an official foreign policy goal. You can argue, for example, that the best way we promote freedom is to preserve our own—something we might give some attention to, as it happens. [Conservative columnist] Irving Kristol once quipped—quite profoundly, as usual—that the only successful American foreign policy is immigration.

Ever since [former presidents Jimmy] Carter and [Ronald] Reagan put human rights and democracy, respectively, high on their foreign policy agendas, we have spent a lot of money and expended quite a lot of hot rhetorical air, but achieved very little. It is really as if all the billions spent on and by NED, USAID, the State Department's Human Rights bureau, and the rest have been a transfer payment to middle class Americans much, much more than they have been real crusades, with tangible results, for democracy in unfree countries.

Hillary Clinton, when she was First Lady, visited Tunisia one time when I happened to be there, and she gave support to the regime of Ben Ali, ostentatiously visiting some model housing project in Tunis that, supposedly, represented splendidly his program of gradual improvement. The [Barack] Obama administration only a few weeks ago was congratulating Ben Ali as a partner in the war against terror and a model of orderly economic progress, even if a bit backward in areas like press freedom (there are no independent news media in Tunisia and until the recent riots, the Internet was under tight control). In between, the [George W.] Bush administration took the same line.

There was nothing shocking in these gestures: they represent normal state-to-state courtesies that, unless we want to call into question the whole system of international relations, we can scarcely avoid. But since that is so obviously so, what difference does it make to the Tunisian regime if the State Department, in its annual human rights report, gives it low marks? Or even that the U.S. Embassy, according to a Wikileak document, refers to the joint as a police state? To the defunct regime, all this meant is that we are wimps; to the opposition activists and truth tellers like the imprisoned Taoufik Ben Brik—"the last journalist in Tunisia," as he was known—it can only signify that we are not what we pretend to be.

Jettison the Democracy Promotion Baggage

The point is that purely from a foreign policy perspective, it would be better to jettison the entire democracy-and-human-rights baggage and simply say forthrightly that we, as a nation, support liberty and we wish liberals everywhere a good fight and godspeed, but as a matter of statecraft the issue of freedom outside our borders only becomes part of our strategy when we know it is of clear benefit to us and we expect our policies to have tangible consequences.

In this regard, the 1970s–'80s policy of supporting human rights in the Soviet Union, including the right to emigrate, is exemplary. It became an effective tactic that weakened our adversary, while doing real good to real people. It preceded, and really had nothing to do with, the human rights industry as it developed in certain bureaus of the State Department and associated boondoggles like NED and USAID and their NGO [nongovernmental organization] subcontractors. Indeed, putting pressure on the Soviets on issues of human rights and emigration even preceded the famous [1974] Jackson-Vanik amendment,[1] which in a very real sense was the initial big investment in that industry and thus a terrible precedent.

Regardless—before or after Jackson-Vanik—the point is that pressure was brought to bear on the Soviets as a factor in an overall diplo-politico-military strategy. It was done by ordinary FSOs (Foreign Service Officers), not by specialists in a featherbed called the NED, or even the Bureau of Human Rights. Why does the State Department need such a bureau? Every FSO, every ambassador, is a representative of democ-

1. An amendment to federal law that put pressure on the former Soviet Union to allow minorities and dissidents to emigrate.

racy, of the Republic of Liberty. By bureaucratizing freedom, we simply obfuscate our message.

Democracy Promotion in the Muslim World

Our "democracy promotion" policy toward the Arab-Muslim world demonstrates the bankruptcy of our programs to a sickening extent. Not a single Arab-Muslim country has become more liberal since the instigation of these official foreign policy goals during the Carter and Reagan administrations. The slight gains registered in some countries—Morocco made small gains in women's rights, for example, Algeria has a press that is much freer than it was during the [Hovari] Boumediene years [1963–1978], Kuwait has made some overall gains, as has Qatar—owe nothing, absolutely nothing, to programs funded by any branch, or quasi-branch, of the U.S. government. By contrast, Lebanon has failed as a free country, whereas prior to the Carter and Reagan years it was probably the freest Arab country.

Pakistan, a non-Arab Muslim country, was relatively cool and laid-back prior to our official democracy industry. It is now a land of hysterical madmen, one of the craziest and most dangerous places on earth.

Are these anarchic and tyrannous societies our fault? Of course not. Is it the fault of our democracy industry? Of course not. But has the democracy industry done any good? No. Might there have been more progress in liberalizing the Arab-Muslim world without the democracy industry? Possibly—because our policy would not have been a bundle of contradictions with half-educated bureaucrats tripping all over one another, wasting money, trying to carry out incoherent policy directives, always finally more concerned about their own careers (doing well while doing good is the cynical Washington quip) than in their putative mission.

By coincidence, the Obama administration just released an official review of U.S. foreign aid policy, what we call soft power.

The Quadrennial Diplomacy and Development Review on foreign aid proposes, essentially, to continue the policy of throwing money at ex-colonial countries and looking the other way when it is pocketed by the thugs that run them.

USAID, under the proposed spending, would see its budget increase into the $20 billion stratosphere, while its staff would grow by 5,500, more than doubling its current level. The historical record is that the more money is given to soft power agencies, the more paper these agencies generate in Washington, and the less democracy and clean water systems get to Africa.

The NED Arab programs for years were big, at least on paper, on gender equality. Tunisia, as it happens, always made women's rights one of the cover stories for its success. We may not have the freest political system in the world, the line went, but look at our emancipated women. Incrementally, and supposedly with help from our programs, this was also supposed to be the trend in places like Morocco and Egypt, one-man autocracies where U.S. leaders, with appropriate cheering from the democracists, always managed to find silver linings amid leaden skies.

But any visitor to an Arab country over the years can tell you that the trend seems to be toward veils and even burqas; and outside the few "liberated" neighborhoods in the toniest zones of Tunis or Cairo or Marrakesh, the only ones our democracy missionaries dare visit, the status of women in Arab countries is scarcely a matter for celebration by feminists or democrats. Throughout the Algerian civil war, when school teachers, women's rights advocates, journalists, and democratic trade union leaders were fighting for their lives against an Islamist insurgency, the social democrats at NED lifted nary a finger.

In any event, notwithstanding the billions budgeted for items like "rule of law" and "election processes" and "civil society" and "women's rights," one has only to glance at the arc of crisis stretching across the northern third of Africa to see the success of our approach to the battle for hearts and minds in the vast and perilous region where Arab Islam and black Africa meet. We were never very good in this sphere, and since the demise of Soviet imperialism we have got worse.

America Is Losing Face and Influence

Our ineptitude is viewed by Africans as cynicism, and it breeds contempt. They increasingly turn to the Chinese, who make it clear that if they provide a quo, they expect a quid. The Chinese get natural resources that their expanding industries and growing consumer sector demand. The Africans get infrastructure development—road, rail, sanitation systems.

If there are gains in "good governance" on the side, so much the better, but this is never the Chinese sales pitch. They helped the Khartoum regime, and now they are already offering to help the new regime in Juba, capital of the new nation of South Sudan, and they are not wringing their hands about free and fair elections and human rights.

On the other side of North Africa, there lies another example of the cynicism of our democracy policies. In 1975, the Spaniards withdrew from their Colorado-sized slice of the Sahara, wedged on the Atlantic coast between Algeria, Morocco, and Mauritania. The natives were promised a free and fair election to determine their status, but the U.S., notwithstanding its steadfast support for this U.N.-endorsed position, has never tried to enforce it.

The result has been one of the longest stand-offs in African affairs, 15 years of guerrilla war followed by 20 years of diplomatic stalemate. Just before Christmas the two sides—the

Moroccan government and the representatives of the native tribes (called Sahrawis)—agreed to reconvene (on Long Island) for further talks "soon."

The American interest, at a minimum, ought to be to keep [the Muslim terrorist group al-]Qaeda out of Africa and to go mano-a-mano [hand-to-hand, in direct competition] with the Chinese for the Continent's hearts and minds—and resources. This would be to everyone's advantage—political and economic competition and let the best win.

However, it appears America's Africanists prefer to forfeit the game. From one administration to the other, we waffle and demur. On the question of the Western Sahara, we nod one year toward Morocco's policy of de facto annexation (called autonomy), the next toward self-determination through free-and-fair elections. The Sahrawis, living in shabby dignity in the territory or in refugee areas across the border in Algeria, are, in the minds of our democracists, as Navajos and Cheyennes were in the glory days of the Bureau of Indian Affairs, valuable mainly for jobs they create in Washington.

Time to Pack Up and Go Home

South of the Sahara, we tut-tut as free-and-fair elections are shown up for a complete farce in the Ivory Coast. Since the second round in the November presidential election in that little jewel of a West African nation, two claimants to the palace, I mean the presidency, have dug in their heels: the incumbent Laurent Gbagbo and his rival, Alassane Ouattara, who served as prime minister late in the long rule of the country's first president-for-life-in-all-but-name, Felix Houphouet-Boigny.

The country's Constitutional Council gave the nod to Gbagbo, the Electoral Commission said Ouattara won. The truth is that no one, at present, can honestly say who received more votes. Ouattara may have won in the Muslim north, where he has his base. Gbagbo may have kept his, which is in the Christian-traditionalist south.

When, as a young school teacher and social-democrat, Gbagbo was thrown in jail by the old dictator, his prime minister did not say a word. Neither did our Sunday-school democracists say much, either. It is difficult for a man like Gbagbo—one of the first Africans to support us in the war on terror—to believe our protestations on the importance of free-and-fair are sincere. His rival served the dictator, who kept crocodile pits handy for people who really got on his nerves.

Washington, traditionally, has looked to Paris to get the script on Côte d'Ivoire, and the French prefer Ouattara. He is *comme-il-faut* [the conventional choice], he knows the presidents of major Western countries, and he is a former ranking official of the IMF [International Monetary Fund]. Gbagbo was a working man and a democrat when, due to Cold War priorities, we really did not think that was the in thing in Africa.

None of this necessarily means much in trying to understand the political situation in the Ivory Coast, mind you, but it gives the free-and-fair protestations an off-key sound. If neither USAID nor NED was able to promote a calm and serene free-and-fair in little Ivory Coast any more than in tiny Tunisia, why do they need budget increases? Why not just pack up and go home? And since we never helped, why are we now acting like bullies in telling the Ivoirians who their president is?

The Ivory vote was required by a French-brokered 2007 agreement to reunite a country divided by civil war in 2003, Houphouet's successors having been incapable of maintaining two quite distinct regions together. Reunion will accomplish the opposite of the desired outcome in Sudan: reimpose the colonial borders. The Ivory Coast south of Bouake is preponderantly Catholic, dominated by Baole and Bete tribes whose outlook is shaped by the commercial culture of coastal West Africa. To the north, the savannahs blend into the Sahel, the long "coast" along the Sahara's southern shore that stretches from the Atlantic to north Sudan and the Red Sea. People here come from Burkina Faso (ex Upper Volta), or their families did, and they read the Koran rather than the Bible.

Let Them Find Freedom on Their Own

This is all very sad but it is also very dangerous. From Sudan to the Western Sahara, passing by the tottering Ben Ali and the impossible situation in the Ivory Coast, we see an arc or crisis that, if it snaps, will benefit our enemies. The Sahara represents an almost impenetrable sanctuary for the jihadists who call themselves AQIM—al Qaeda in the Islamic Maghreb. These are serious killers, as they demonstrate every now and then. Most recently, a brazen kidnap-murder operation against French development workers took place in downtown Niamey, a laid back city in Niger where no one expected trouble. The French sent a commando unit to hunt down this gang, but there are many more where they come from.

AQIM follows an all-points strategy, probing for opportunities in every direction. Our response is to sing the free-and-fair elections mantra, and not even consistently. Sudan always was two countries—why the wasted time and effort when a policy of forthright support for the South would have by now got us a base in one of the most strategic locations on the Continent, opposite the Middle East and astride Arab and black Africa? On the Atlantic side, effective control of the Western Sahara surely weighs more than who is the nominal sovereign—the people who live there or the sultan of Morocco—so why not just do whatever needs doing, instead of broadcasting that our talk of exporting democracy is a cynical sham?

If past experience is any guide, Ben Ali having gone the way of the Shah [of Iran; i.e., ousted], our democracists have made it as likely as not that Tunisian democrats have just enough time to thank us for nothing before the resurgent Islamists sweep them away.

As to the Ivory Coast, instead of quietly letting its two halves devolve from the center that only the old dictator could hold, and then letting the separate socio-cultural entities find their way back naturally into some kind of federal arrangement that could be a bastion of pro-Americanism in a key region between the oil-rich Gulf of Guinea and the Sahel, we are risking a catastrophe on the scale of the Nigeria-Biafra war. Which none of our democracists even remember.

The [Woodrow] Wilsonian idea of promoting American interests by making the world safe for democracy is not without merit, but it is difficult to see where it has been implemented effectively since Jimmy Carter and Ronald Reagan, each in his own way, gave the world the notion that the U.S. places human rights and democracy at the center of its foreign policy. The question should be asked whether this has been a historic mistake. Liberal democracy really does not have much of a record outside the English-speaking lands. We can promote freedom far more effectively than we can our culturally bound systems of liberal democratic governance, based as it is on the rule of law, property rights, and so forth. But freedom means letting people go their way and not sending them cynical signals about democratic standards that lead to perdition [damnation].

> "We [in AFRICOM] . . . have found that our own national interest in a stable and prosperous Africa is shared strongly by our African partners."

AFRICOM Will Help Ensure African Security

Robert Moeller

In the following viewpoint, Robert Moeller claims that the US Africa Command (AFRICOM) was established with the intention of promoting US interests on the continent and helping African nations improve their own security. In Moeller's opinion, AFRICOM has no plans to increase its military presence in Africa and is not in a position to dictate policy in any nation. Instead, he insists the organization trains African security forces and helps coordinate cross-border projects to quell piracy and militant extremism when these forces threaten regional peace. Moeller is a retired vice admiral in the US Navy. From October 2007 to April 2010, he served as the first deputy to the commander for military operations, US Africa Command.

As you read, consider the following questions:

1. As Moeller reports, about how much of the US government ment spending on Africa is channeled to military projects on the continent?

2. Where is the headquarters of AFRICOM, as Moeller reveals?

3. According to the author, what percentage of international peacekeeping forces in Africa today are from African nations?

I feel fortunate that I can say that I was present at the inception of U.S. Africa Command (Africom), the U.S. military headquarters that oversees and coordinates U.S. military activities in Africa. Starting with just a handful of people sitting around a table nearly four years ago [in 2006], we built an organization dedicated to the idea that U.S. security interests in Africa are best served by building long-term partnerships with African nations, regional organizations, and the African Union. At the same time, however, there has been a great deal of speculation and concern about Africom. We believe our work and accomplishments will continue to speak for themselves.

Still, many of these concerns raise important issues, and it is important to continue to address and clarify Africom's position on these issues. There is great work being done by and for Africa nations with Africom's assistance, and the success of the missions between these partner nations inevitably affects the security of the United States and the world as a whole. During our work in designing Africom and helping guide it through the early years of its existence, a number of lessons have helped inform our decisions and ensure we performed our job responsibly and effectively.

Africom Does Not Create Policy

One of the most serious criticisms leveled at Africom is that the organization represents a U.S. military takeover of the foreign-policy process. This is certainly not true, though I suspect some of our more outspoken critics have been so vocal about this that it is quite challenging for them to change course.

Let there be no mistake. Africom's job is to protect American lives and promote American interests. That is what nations and militaries do. But we also have found that our own national interest in a stable and prosperous Africa is shared strongly by our African partners. By working together, we can pursue our shared interests more effectively.

Africa's security challenges are well known. They include piracy and illegal trafficking, ethnic tensions, irregular militaries and violent extremist groups, undergoverned regions, and pilferage of resources. This last challenge includes oil theft, as well as widespread illegal fishing that robs the African people of an estimated $1 billion a year because their coastal patrols lack the capacity to find and interdict suspicious vessels within their territorial waters and economic exclusion zones.

As a military organization, most of our work consists of supporting security and stability programs in Africa and its island nations. Our focus is on building capacity, both with African national militaries and, increasingly, with Africa's regional organizations. One of our biggest success stories is the Africa Partnership Station, a Navy program that partners Africom with African and international sailors to put together a multinational staff aboard a U.S. or international vessel. This creates what some have called a "floating schoolhouse," where the staff share a host of ideas, ranging from basic search-and-rescue techniques to advanced concepts of maritime domain awareness.

Across the continent, we work closely within the framework of the overall U.S. government effort. As a military organization, we do not create policy. Rather, we support those policy decisions and coordinate our actions closely with the State Department, U.S. embassies in the region, the U.S.

Agency for International Development (USAID), and other U.S. government agencies that have been trusted partners in Africa for decades.

Africom Works with the Diplomatic Corps

It's no secret that Africom's early rollout was met by concern within some quarters of the foreign-policy community. We've worked hard to allay those concerns. Despite the warnings of skeptics, the past three years have not seen any dramatic increase in numbers of U.S. personnel or military funding directed at Africa. Depending on how you count the figures, the U.S. military represents between 5 and 10 percent of all U.S government spending in Africa, and we do not anticipate significant future shifts. We believe diplomacy, development, and defense should work hand in hand—and in balance—to achieve long-term security. Defense Secretary Robert Gates has spoken eloquently about the need to increase funding for diplomacy and development and has warned of what he calls "excessive militarization."

The U.S. military has been working with African militaries for decades, but the work was not sustained and integrated as effectively as it probably could have been to complement and better support the activities of other agencies of the U.S. government. In many ways, Africom was devised as a test platform for helping the military as an institution to better understand its role in supporting diplomacy and development. State Department and USAID officials serve in senior billets on the staff, advising the military on the best way to support their agencies. And yes, they frequently send message traffic back to their home offices to help ensure the military understands its subordinate role in Africa.

All the U.S. military's work in Africa is done with the approval of U.S. ambassadors. We take that seriously. I have seen anecdotal stories of military personnel showing up in an African nation unaware that they ultimately report to the U.S.

The AFRICOM Mission

We seek to be a friend to the continent of Africa, its nations and its institutions. All of our efforts focus on adding value to our engagement efforts and not disrupting, nor confusing the ongoing US Government or international programmes.

The vision for AFRICOM is that 10, 20 years from now, there is a continent of Africa that is stable, whose governments perform legitimately, whose security structures help assure its national treasures to be used for the betterment of its people.

William E. Ward, Military Technology, January 2009.

ambassador of the host nation in question. If you run across one of those stories, take a look at the date. There's a strong chance that incident took place before or not long after October 2008, when Africom formally became responsible for everything the U.S. military does in Africa. One of the reasons Africom was created was to help put an end to that kind of confusion.

A Limited Footprint in Africa

We have also been accused of looking to establish military bases across the African continent. This was false when the rumors arose at the time of Africom's creation and remains false today. Africom's headquarters is in Stuttgart, Germany, and we are not looking for any other location. Misconceptions arose when, in the early months of 2007, some people in the U.S. Defense Department community considered the idea of positioning small teams regionally to better coordinate the command's day-to-day partnerships. However, there was never a formal search, and as soon as the command opened its doors in October 2007, we made it clear that we intended to stay in Stuttgart for the foreseeable future.

Our footprint in Africa remains purposefully limited. We have only one forward operating base, at Camp Lemonnier in Djibouti, established in 2002 under the U.S. Central Command. In 2008, Africom inherited the base, which is an ideal site for supporting our military-to-military programs across eastern Africa and also serves as a key node in the Defense Department's global transportation infrastructure. We are not seeking any additional bases.

We also have a few dozen program officers and liaisons working across the continent, mainly in U.S. embassies. This hardly means, however, that we are building "mini-Africom headquarters" in U.S. embassies, as some have suggested. What we've done is send one or two staff officers to join embassy teams so that our diplomats do not have to spend their time coordinating military programs. It is common practice world-wide for a small number of military personnel to play a sup-porting role in a larger diplomatic mission. Our ambassadors continue to be the president's personal representatives within each nation.

Listening to Africans

We have spent the last three years meeting with African lead-ers, African media, and African people. Mostly, we have been listening. And what we have heard is that many people across Africa have an interest in long-term stability.

The consistent message we hear from the leadership and the people of Africa is that they want to provide for their own security. Despite sometimes difficult histories, many African nations today are working to develop professional security forces that follow the rule of law and protect all their peoples. African nations today make up more than 40 percent of all international peacekeepers deployed throughout Africa with the United Nations and African Union. Their goal is for Africans to make up 100 percent of the peacekeeping forces within Africa. By building a regionally focused African Standby Force, the African Union seeks to play an ever-greater role in bringing peace and security to turbulent regions on the continent.

Rather than deploying large numbers of U.S. military forces, we accomplish our goals by conducting hundreds of what we refer to as "capacity-building" events each year. Africom sends small teams of specialists to dozens of countries to offer our perspective on military topics such as leadership, the importance of civilian control of the military, the importance of an inspector general program, the finer points of air-traffic control and port security, aircraft maintenance, military law, and squad tactics for a unit preparing for peacekeeping deployment or patrols against violent extremist groups—the list goes on. Even though we are showing and explaining how we do business, we are not imposing U.S. methods upon our partners. After all, our practices might not be right for them—that is a question they must answer, based on the information they receive not only from us, but from their many international partners.

We also take part in military exercises that promote cross-border cooperation and coordination. We participated in Exercise Flintlock this May [2010], which was designed to help nations in West and North Africa cooperate more effectively on cross-border threats from illegal traffickers and violent extremist groups. Another exercise, Africa Endeavor, brought together 25 African nations in Gabon to coordinate their communications technology. This is a surprisingly challenging task, due to the fact that this diverse array of nations uses a hodgepodge of computers and radios made in different countries throughout the world. Not only do these exercises solve practical problems—they provide former adversaries or strangers with opportunities to develop a shared history of working together to solve problems. This year's Africa Endeavor exercise is scheduled to take place in Ghana, and we are expecting 30 nations to be involved.

Do Not Expect Instant Results

Our partners in Africa warn us that we must adopt an "African time" perspective. We should not expect quick results or approach the continent with a "make it happen now" mindset. At the same time, we do see slow, steady progress. Coups are decreasingly tolerated as a means of acceptable regime change, and in some cases, such as Mauritania, we have seen militaries take stock of the international community and make steady progress in restoring civil authority. Much of our work is aimed at reinforcing African success stories so that we can work together as capable partners to address regional and global concerns. Tensions in Sudan as next year's referendum on southern independence approaches can be reduced if regional neighbors build cooperative relationships with all parties in Sudan.

Somalia remains a country in daily conflict, with a people so fiercely proud of their independence that any lasting security solution must be African-led. As I write this, the Ugandan People's Defense Force is operating deep inside neighboring nations, with an unprecedented level of intergovernmental cooperation, to end the decades-long reign of terror by the Lord's Resistance Army, an extremist group that has killed tens of thousands and displaced millions.

In the Democratic Republic of the Congo, the U.S. military is one small player in a much larger international effort to help that nation reform its security sector. We have provided some funding to renovate medical facilities that provide support to survivors of sexual and gender-based violence, and we are currently conducting a six-month pilot project to train a model military unit in the Congolese Army. Although this program includes basic military skills training, it also emphasizes respect for human rights, the rule of law, and an understanding of the military's role in a civil society.

As we conduct our daily and weekly activities across Africa we believe we share a long-term vision with our African partners: Sustained security programs can, over time, help support the conditions for economic development, social development, and improvements in health—so that people will continue to see progress in their lives and growing prosperity in their communities.

That is how we support U.S. foreign policy in Africa, while also promoting the long-term aspirations of the African people. It has indeed been a personal honor and a privilege to be a part of the creation of Africom.

"*[AFRICOM] has stirred fears of American hegemony and the militarisation of the US relationship with Africa.*"

AFRICOM Will Likely Serve Only US Interests in Africa

Ed Blanche

In the following viewpoint, Ed Blanche asserts that while the mission of the US Africa Command (AFRICOM) is to help train African security forces and facilitate peacekeeping on the continent, many in Africa and the United States question the military's true motives. Blanche claims that the United States already has used covert military forces to help subvert governments in Africa, and he fears AFRICOM will become another strike force to protect US interests such as oil production in key African states. Even if this is not the case and AFRICOM presently has no military agenda, Blanche wonders how long it will be before these American troops get entangled in wars over oil or other vital resources in short supply. Blanche is a journalist and a member of the International Institute for Strategic Studies in London.

As you read, consider the following questions:

1. As Blanche writes, what congressional committee expressed concern in 2008 about extending US military reach into Africa?

2. In what African country does the author say the US Combined Joint Task Force already has a base of operations?

3. According to Blanche, what African country's stable government was overthrown by a cross-border attack aided by US commando forces?

The headquarters of America's controversial new military command in Africa, known in military parlance as Africom, the structure through which the US will conduct "strategic engagement" with a continent it long ignored, was inaugurated on 1 October 2008. But the omens are not good.

Only Liberia was prepared to host the new HQ, but even the Americans, desperate to find an African base for Africom, found Liberia a bit shaky and so passed on that. Every other African country gave it a miss. So for the foreseeable future—and perhaps for as long as the new command functions—Africom is based in the German city of Stuttgart, several thousands of miles from Africa's northern boundary along the Mediterranean Sea.

AFRICOM's Size and Mission

Africom will coordinate all US military activity across Africa and is responsible for military relations with 53 African countries, excluding Egypt. Until Africom came along, US military involvement in Africa was split between the US European Command in Germany, the Florida-based Central Command which covers the Middle East and Central Asia, and the Pacific Command in Hawaii.

Africom's physical presence on the ground is expected to be small—primarily training groups—and its military assets relatively light, but the new command has stirred fears of American hegemony and the militarisation of the US relationship with Africa. General William Ward, Africom's first commander, has said that the new command has "no hidden agenda", that its objective is to help Africans solve their own problems, carry out peacekeeping and humanitarian missions, and help train the continent's armies to maintain stability and order. But US aid organisations that are active in Africa, and even the US Congress, aghast at the Pentagon's astronomical spending and budgetary demands because of Iraq and Afghanistan, is questioning that.

A US Military Presence in Africa

In July 2008, senior members of the congressional Subcommittee on National Security and Foreign Affairs of the House Oversight Committee expressed deep scepticism, bordering on outright anger, at the US military's plans to expand its global reach into Africa. They felt Africom's primary mission was to ensure access to Africa's growing oil production, counter China's swelling inroads into the continent for oil, minerals and investment, and to smother terrorism. The committee's chairman, John Tierney, a Massachusetts Democrat, cautioned that if the aim was to help Africans overcome their problems, why was the US sending the military? "Who is going to buy that?" he asked.

To Tierney, "it looks like [Africom] is going over there to protect oil and fight terrorists, the same misguided way that we fought terrorists in other places. What would be the reaction in Washington if China or Russia established a military 'outpost' in Africa?" he asked. According to the US Government Accountability Office, Africom will cost around $4bn [billion] between 2010 and 2015. That includes $2bn for the 1,800-strong Combined Joint Task Force, a counter-terrorism outfit, based at an old Foreign Legion camp in Djibouti. At this point, that is the only long-term US military facility in Africa.

In September 2008, the House of Representatives empha-
sised its scepticism by voting to allocate $266m [million] to
Africom for its first years of operations—$123m less than
former President George [W.] Bush had requested. The House
Appropriations Committee explained that the reduction was
imposed largely because of "the failure to establish an American presence on the continent."

Under Bush's military-dominated foreign policy, the Pentagon (or Department of Defence) became more the driver of
policymaking than the State Department, and this caused
widespread concern not just in the US but among America's
allies. The cynicism of the Bush administration was amply un-
derlined in early 2007 when it unveiled its plans to set up Africom, for what the deputy under-secretary for defence, Teresa
Whalen, explained was aimed at "promoting security, to build
African capacity to develop their own environment and not be
subject to the instability that has toppled governments and
caused so much pain on the continent."

Clandestine US Operations

Yet only weeks before, the Bush administration had clandes-
tinely masterminded the overthrow of Somalia's first stable
government in 16 years, dominated by the Islamist Courts
Union, which was viewed as a threat by the Americans.

US commandos spearheaded the Ethiopia invasion of Somalia in the last two weeks of 2006, hardwired with satellite
and electronic surveillance intelligence, to re-install the feeble,
UN-backed Transnational Federal Government, made up of
rival warlords and their proxies.

Elsewhere, the explosive situation in Nigeria's oil regions
has not abated, with the kidnapping of foreign oil workers going on all the time. Presumably, to protect US energy supplies,
Africom would be Washington's military instrument to ensure
the oil keeps flowing. General Ward says his command has no

Militarizing Corrupt Regimes

America's flawed understanding and obsession with terrorism has led to a foreign policy of militarization throughout Africa. These military programs, now consolidated under Africom, comprise a great threat to African peace, security, democracy and sovereignty. Training and weapons are being provided to phantom, failed, corrupt, and undemocratic regimes. . . . Some of these countries' civil liberties ratings declined, and human rights condition deteriorated considerably after 2007. Chad and Mauritania, two countries supported by the Pentagon's Program have experienced military coup d'etat [overthrow of the government]. American anti-terrorist programs are supporting and legitimating criminal governments who often terrorize their own people with impunity. It consolidates African governments' coercive and repressive apparatus and its capacity to resist domestic opponents' demands for a full democratization.

Gilbert L. Taguem Fah,
Journal of Pan African Studies, *March 2010.*

plans to build permanent bases across Africa. But if Africom ever sets up headquarters in Africa, that will likely be a permanent installation.

Still, the US seeks to establish access to military facilities—primarily airfields and naval depots—in each of Africa's five regions. But it is the use of the Combined Joint Task Force-Horn of Africa (CTF-HOA) in operations against Somalia's Islamists that has exacerbated African fears that Africom's agenda may extend beyond humanitarian and training missions. For the time being at least, Africom is pretty much a naval affair on the premise that US ground forces could undermine key US interests in Africa and that naval initiatives are less intrusive. The naval presence is currently built around the Africa Partnership Station (APS), with US warships deploying from the European Command to promote maritime security and safety by building up African naval capabilities.

The 17,000-ton amphibious transport ship USS *Nashville* has been carrying the Africom flag. This Austin-class vessel arrived in the Gulf of Guinea in January 2008 and visited Senegal, Ghana, Nigeria, Cameroon and Gabon during a five-month deployment. For now, the APS is focusing on West and Central Africa, in particular the Gulf of Guinea, the heart of West Africa's oil industry.

Protecting Oil and Other US Interests

Two Gulf of Guinea states, São Tomé & Príncipe and Equatorial Guinea (especially its Malabo archipelago), are possible contenders for Africom naval facilities. Both of these island clusters have major advantages for the Americans because they cover key shipping routes and West Africa's burgeoning oil industry.

Nigeria—one of Africa's leading oil producers and economic powers—and the US have common interests in bolstering regional security. Nigeria is the fifth largest oil supplier to the US, providing some two million barrels of crude per day.

More than half of that comes from the Niger Delta, but anti-government forces have been steadily forcing production cutbacks through constant attacks on oil facilities, on land and offshore in the Gulf of Guinea, in an escalating conflict that threatens both states. All told, the US currently gets nearly one quarter of its oil from West Africa.

The Gulf of Guinea is the epicentre of new oil reserves that are being developed by Nigeria and its neighbours, including Ghana. Most of that oil will be destined for the US, with tankers loading from offshore platforms and sailing directly across the Atlantic to terminals on the US eastern seaboard. Strategically, this is of major importance to the Americans since those shipments of crude are not exposed to disruption in the way that supplies from the volatile Middle East are.

So, improving maritime security in the Gulf of Guinea, and other areas, is of supreme importance to the US and the oil-rich African countries in the area. And with the prospect that the wars of the coming decades will be fought primarily over the planet's dwindling resources, Africom may find itself locked into conflicts in Africa that leave little, if any, room for the peacekeeping and humanitarian missions it says are its primary functions.

Periodical Bibliography

The following articles have been selected to supplement the diverse views presented in this chapter.

Catherine Besteman   "'Beware of Those Bearing Gifts': An Anthropologist's View of AFRICOM," *Anthropology Today*, October 2008.

Emmanuel Bombande   "The Way Ahead for AFRICOM," *Journal of International Peace Operations*, March/April 2009.

Colleen C. Denny and Ezekiel J. Emanuel   "US Health Aid Beyond PEPFAR," *JAMA: Journal of the American Medical Association*, November 5, 2008.

Gilbert L. Taguem Fah   "Dealing with AFRICOM: The Political Economy of Anger and Protest," *Journal of Pan African Studies*, March 2010.

Peter Navario   "PEPFAR's Biggest Success Is Also Its Largest Liability," *Lancet*, July 18, 2009.

Barack Obama   "Africa Is a Fundamental Part of Our Interconnected World," *Vital Speeches of the Day*, July 2009.

Lisa Smith   "PEPFAR 2: Fighting HIV/AIDS (and Human Nature)," *Humanist*, May/June 2008.

Rochelle P. Walensky and Daniel R. Kuritzkes   "The Impact of the President's Emergency Plan for AIDS Relief (PEPFAR) Beyond HIV and Why It Remains Essential," *Clinical Infectious Diseases*, January 15, 2010.

Nicolas van de Walle   "US Policy Towards Africa: The Bush Legacy and the Obama Administration," *African Affairs*, January 2010.

William E. Ward   "Engaging AFRICOM," *Military Technology*, January 2009.

For Further Discussion

Chapter 1

1. Compare the kinds of evidence Charles Kenny and Bruce Gilley use to make their arguments about the fortunes of Africa in the early twenty-first century. Whose argument do you find more persuasive? Explain why, and be sure to specify which examples from the text you found most convincing. Why do you believe it is important that the world should either be more optimistic or pessimistic about the state of Africa in the new millennium?

2. After reading the viewpoints by Marian L. Tupy and Gregory Elich, explain what you believe are the strengths and drawbacks of expanding free trade in Africa. What kind of trade policies do you think would best suit a small African economy? Cite from the articles to support your opinion.

3. Helene Gallis argues that African ingenuity—born of necessity—is creating sustainable business practices that might be good models for developed countries to emulate. Why do you think such practices work in Africa? Do you believe these community-based businesses and "heirloom design" strategies could or should be adopted in developed counties? WHy or why not? What would be the advantages and disadvantages?

Chapter 2

1. In the past decade, several critics have argued that foreign aid in Africa is doing more harm than good. Reread the viewpoint by Mathew K. Jallow and then restate what you understand to be the main points of this anti-aid view. Do you think cutting off or curtailing foreign aid will

benefit Africa in the long run, or do you believe, like Scott Baldauf, that aid has helped Africa and should continue for the foreseeable future? Explain your answer.

2. After reading the first four viewpoints in this chapter, devise a method of foreign assistance that would help African nations without fear of graft or other concerns about its disbursement to the people in need. In your answer, consider these questions: Who should deliver this aid (governments, nongovernmental organizations, or private charities)? Who should receive the aid? What kinds of aid should be given (and what kinds should be restricted)? What conditions (if any) would you place on this aid disbursement?

3. Andrew M. Mwenda charges Western nations with unjustly managing how African nations should develop. He maintains that each African nation is different and possesses its own trials and successes, yet Western governments tend to insist on devising an economic policy "blueprint" to cover all of Africa. Do you think Mwenda's charge is accurate? Are Western nations too meddlesome in African countries' paths toward development? If you were the president of the United States, how would you respond to Mwenda's assertion?

Chapter 3

1. Michael Fumento makes the argument that the AIDS epidemic in Africa has been knowingly overblown. What evidence does he cite to promote his opinion, and why does he believe AIDS organizations would perpetuate this overstatement? Do you find his arguments convincing? Explain.

2. After reading the viewpoints in this chapter, enumerate what you think are the most significant contributors to the spread of AIDS in Africa. Which of these concerns do you think is the most pressing, and how would you ad-

dress this problem if you were the chief health official in a sub-Saharan African nation where the disease was rampant?

3. Do you think Africa will soon bring the spread of AIDS under control? After reading the articles in this chapter, explain what positive signs you see that would make you believe the disease may be contained in the next ten or twenty years. Alternatively, if you doubt the disease will be controlled in coming decades, what factors do you think ensure its widespread transmission?

Chapter 4

1. Russ Feingold maintains that America has a duty to promote democracy in African nations to safeguard human rights and peace. Roger Kaplan argues that US foreign policy has achieved little in terms of promoting democracy. He claims that the United States has backed tyrants in the name of democracy promotion and kept Africans from pursuing their own course toward freedom. After reviewing both viewpoints, explain whose argument you find more convincing. Explain what details that author used to persuade you to agree with his opinion.

2. Robert Moeller claims that AFRICOM is a peaceful organization that serves African nations by training security forces to deal with terrorism, extremism, and piracy. Ed Blanche doubts AFRICOM's stated intentions. Although the organization may not currently place many US military personnel in Africa, he fears that establishing bases in Africa is simply a means to facilitate the protection of vital US interests (such as African oil) if the need arises. Based on the evidence given in these viewpoints and any other articles you can find on the topic, what do you believe are the true intentions of AFRICOM? Be sure to explain what arguments or past events convince you of your opinion.

Organizations to Contact

The editors have compiled the following list of organizations concerned with the issues debated in this book. The descriptions are derived from materials provided by the organizations. All have publications or information available for interested readers. The list was compiled on the date of publication of the present volume; the information provided here may change. Be aware that many organizations take several weeks or longer to respond to inquiries, so allow as much time as possible.

Africa Action
1634 Eye St. NW, Ste. 1000, Washington, DC   20006
(202) 546-7961 • fax: (202) 546-1545
e-mail: info@africaaction.org
website: www.africaaction.org

Africa Action is a national organization promoting US government policy that aids in the achievement of peace and development in Africa. Through educational provisions and public awareness programs, the organization seeks to ensure fair treatment and equal opportunity for those living in Africa. Africa Action publishes the annual report *Africa Policy Outlook* and offers other resources such as talking points and fact sheets on its website.

African Union (AU)
PO Box 3243, Addis Ababa
   Ethiopia
+251 11 551 77 00 • fax: +251 11 551 78 44
website: www.au.int/en

Established in 1999 as the Organization of African Unity, the African Union provides a central organizing body to address the continent's most pressing problems. Over time, the work of the AU has focused on issues such as the effects of postcolonization and apartheid, increasing development, and unification of African countries while still observing national sovereignty. The organization's website houses various reports from the member councils.

AVERT

4 Brighton Rd., Horsham, West Sussex   RF13 5BA
  United Kingdom
+44 (0)1403 210202
e-mail: info@avert.org
website: www.avert.org

The international AIDS charity AVERT works to reduce the number of and impact of HIV/AIDS infections globally through education and promotion of positive, proactive treatment of the disease. Many of the organization's projects focus on Africa and India, with an emphasis on prevention as well as aid for those already impacted by AIDS. AVERT's website offers regional summaries of the AIDS epidemic as well as more detailed, specific reports about the prevalence of the disease within particular countries such as South Africa, Malawi, and Uganda.

Cato Institute

1000 Massachusetts Ave. NW, Washington, DC   20001-5403
(202) 842-0200 • fax: (202) 842-3490
website: www.cato.org

The Cato Institute, a nonprofit, public policy research organization promoting the principles of libertarianism, analyzes all aspects of the US government's domestic and foreign policy, offers recommendations to policy makers, and educates the public on current issues debated in the government. One project of the institute, the Center for Global Liberty and Prosperity, studies the problems faced by developing nations, and promotes free market solutions as the best option to combat these problems. The center publishes the annual report *Economic Freedom of the World* as well as the periodic newsletter *Economic Development Bulletin*.

Economic Commission for Africa (ECA)

PO Box 3001, Addis Ababa
  Ethiopia
+251 11 551 7200 • fax: +251 11 551 2233
e-mail: ecainfo@uneca.org
website: www.uneca.org

The Economic Commission for Africa is a regional agency of the United Nations focusing on economic and social development within Africa. The commission works in cooperation with the African Union to implement programs that benefit the individual countries of Africa as well as the continent as a whole. Additionally, ECA focuses on the specific needs of African countries, especially with regard to poverty, growth and development, and gender issues. Publications of the ECA include the annual *Economic Report on Africa*, as well as *Governance for a Progressing Africa*, and *Striving for Good Governance in Africa*.

Foundation for Democracy in Africa

1200 G St. NW, Ste. 800, Washington, DC   20004
(202) 331-1333 • fax: (202) 331-8547
e-mail: webmaster@democracy-africa.org
website: www.democracy-africa.org

The Foundation for Democracy in Africa operates as a nongovernmental organization with consultative status in the United Nations Economic and Social Council. The foundation works to promote programs in Africa that operate on and proliferate the fundamental principles of democracy and free market economics. Additionally, it seeks to help existing African democracies establish themselves within the global economy. The foundation's website offers archived issues of the *Africa Growth and Opportunity Act Civil Society Network Newsletter* and the *Western Hemisphere African Diaspora Network Newsletter*.

Human Rights Watch (HRW)

350 Fifth Ave., 34th Fl., New York, NY   10118-3299
(212) 290-4700 • fax: (212) 736-1300
e-mail: hrwnyc@hrw.org
website: www.hrw.org

Human Rights Watch is an international organization dedicated to ensuring that the human rights of individuals worldwide are observed and protected. In order to achieve this protection, HRW investigates allegations of human rights abuses then works to hold violators, be it governments or individuals, accountable for their actions. The organization's website is divided by continent, offering specific information on individual countries and issues. In the Africa section, numerous reports and press releases are available on topics such as the Libyan revolution and dictatorial regimes in West Africa and other countries.

Institute for Human Rights and Development in Africa (IHRDA)

949 Brusubi Layout, AU Summit Highway
PO Box 1896, Banjul
   The Gambia
+220 220 44 10 413/4 • fax: +220 44 10 201
e-mail: ihrda@ihrda.org
website: www.africaninstitute.org

The Institute for Human Rights and Development in Africa is a nongovernmental, pan-African organization striving to increase awareness and accessibility of human rights protection in Africa in coordination with the African Union. The institute works to accomplish this goal through training programs for human rights activists, free legal aid, research, networking, and advocacy. IHRDA published the *Compilation of Decisions of the African Commission,* a book containing text of the decisions of the Assembly of Heads of States and Government of the African Union; other information detailing the African Regional System is available on the organization's website.

International Fund for Agricultural Development (IFAD)

1775 K St. NW, Ste. 410, Washington, DC   20006-1502

(202) 331-9099 • fax: (202) 331-9366

website: www.ifad.org

The International Fund for Agricultural Development is the United Nation's agency focused on combating the effects of rural poverty in developing countries and aiding individuals in poverty in establishing sustainable lifestyles. The organization provides low-interest loans and grants to developing countries' governments and acts as an advocate for the rural impoverished within the international community. IFAD works to educate the public about the effects of poverty and its possible solutions with the publication of reports such as *Rural Poverty Report 2011, Polishing the Stone* (concerning gender equality in rural development), and *Climate Change.* In addition, the organization has created numerous, country-specific fact sheets.

International Monetary Fund (IMF)

700 Nineteenth St. NW, Washington, DC   20431

(202) 623-7300 • fax: (202) 623-6278

e-mail: publicaffairs@imf.org

website: www.imf.org

The International Monetary Fund works to foster international trade to benefit all countries and promote economic cooperation worldwide. The organization also offers financial loans to nations to help these countries develop their economies. IMF collects information on all 185 member countries, both developed and developing nations, and serves as a clearinghouse for current data and statistics regarding the economic standing of these countries. The fund provides numerous fact sheets, pamphlets, and brochures, all of which are available on the organization's website.

Joint United Nations Programme on HIV/AIDS (UNAIDS)

20 Ave. Appia, Geneva   CH-1211
 Switzerland
+41 22 791 4187
website: www.unaids.org

The Joint United Nations Programme on HIV/AIDS coordinates efforts to internationally combat the AIDS epidemic. The organization focuses its efforts on areas such as prevention, treatment, and care; populations most affected by the disease; the broader effects of the disease on communities; and general research into vaccines and preventive measures. UNAIDS publishes numerous documents detailing all aspects of this global disease, with most reports in their extensive catalog available on the organization's website.

Partnership to Cut Hunger and Poverty in Africa

499 S. Capitol St., Ste. 500B, Washington, DC   20003
(202) 479-4501 • fax: (202) 488-0590
e-mail: webresponse@partnership-africa.org
website: www.africanhunger.org

The Partnership to Cut Hunger and Poverty in Africa formed in 2000 as a coalition of Africans and Americans concerned about the impact and prevalence of poverty and famine in Africa. The organization emphasizes the importance of using aid from the West, in particular from the United States, as a tool for ending hunger in Africa. The partnership works to ensure that aid packages are used in beneficial initiatives, such as rural development, to provide lasting results of reduced poverty. The organization's publications include *Now Is the Time: A Plan to Cut Hunger and Poverty in Africa*, *The Right Way to Aid Africa*, and *Beating Africa's Poverty by Investing in Africa's Infrastructure*.

Third World Network Africa (TWN Africa)

9 Ollenu St., East Legon, PO Box AN 19452, Accra-North
 Ghana

+233 243 111 789
website: www.twnafrica.org

Third World Network Africa works to ensure that the rights and needs of Africans are observed and protected on a global scale through research and advocacy efforts. The network focuses on the promotion of sustainable development practices as central to the growth and well-being of individuals in developing countries as well as the importance of equal access to global resources. TWN Africa publishes the bimonthly magazine *African Agenda* and makes available archived issues of the monthly newsletter *African Trade Agenda*.

World Bank
1818 H St. NW, Washington, DC   20433
(202) 473-1000 • fax: (202) 477-6391
website: www.worldbank.org

The World Bank provides monetary assistance to developing countries worldwide in the form of low-interest loans. The money provided is intended to aid these countries in developing their economies and social and political infrastructures in order to reduce poverty on a global level. World Bank money in Africa has aided in the creation of schools and housing, as well as providing the basis for sustainable development and the reduction of HIV/AIDS. Current publications include the *World Development Report 2010* and numerous documents on investment, lending practices, and economic growth in Africa.

Bibliography of Books

George B.N. Ayittey — *Africa Unchained: The Blueprint for Africa's Future.* New York: Palgrave Macmillan, 2006.

Jean-Paul Azam — *Trade, Exchange Rate, and Growth in Sub-Saharan Africa.* New York: Cambridge University Press, 2007.

Elias K. Bongmba — *Facing a Pandemic: The African Church and the Crisis of HIV/AIDS.* Waco, TX: Baylor University Press, 2007.

Patrick Burnett and Firoze Manji, eds. — *From Slave Trade to Free Trade: How Trade Undermines Democracy and Justice in Africa.* Oxford: Fahamu, 2007.

Robert Calderisi — *The Trouble with Africa: Why Foreign Aid Isn't Working.* New York: Palgrave Macmillan, 2006.

Catherine Campbell — *"Letting Them Die": Why HIV/AIDS Prevention Programmes Fail.* Bloomington: Indiana University Press, 2003.

Luc Christiaensen and Lionel Demery — *Down to Earth: Agriculture and Poverty Reduction in Africa.* Washington, DC: World Bank, 2007.

Richard Dowden — *Africa: Altered States, Ordinary Miracles.* New York: PublicAffairs, 2010.

William Easterly   *The White Man's Burden: Why the West's Efforts to Aid the Rest Have Done So Much Ill and So Little Good.* New York: Penguin, 2006.

Helen Epstein   *The Invisible Cure: Africa, the West and the Fight Against AIDS.* New York: Farrar, Straus & Giroux, 2007.

James Ferguson   *Global Shadows: Africa in the Neoliberal World Order.* Durham, NC: Duke University Press, 2006.

Raymond Fisman and Edward Miguel   *Economic Gangsters: Corruption, Violence, and the Poverty of Nations.* Princeton, NJ: Princeton University Press, 2010.

Howard W. French   *A Continent for the Taking: The Tragedy and Hope of Africa.* New York: Knopf, 2004.

John H. Ghazvinian   *Untapped: The Scramble for Africa's Oil.* New York: Harvest, 2007.

David Glenwinkel   *The Insanity of Africa.* Auburn, CA: Village Care International, 2010.

Robert Guest   *The Shackled Continent: Africa's Past, Present and Future.* London: Macmillan, 2004.

Patrick Honohan and Thorsten Beck   *Making Finance Work for Africa.* Washington, DC: World Bank, 2007.

George Klay Kieh Jr., ed.   *Beyond State Failure and Collapse: Making the State Relevant in Africa.* Lanham, MD: Lexington, 2007.

Staffan I. Lindberg · *Democracy and Elections in Africa.* Baltimore: Johns Hopkins University Press, 2006.

Wangari Maathai · *The Challenge for Africa.* New York: Anchor Books, 2010.

Vijay Mahajan · *Africa Rising: How 900 Million African Consumers Offer More than You Think.* Upper Saddle River, NJ: Pearson Education, 2009.

Ama Mazama, ed. · *Africa in the 21st Century: Toward a New Future.* New York: Routledge, 2007.

John Mukum Mbaku · *Corruption in Africa: Causes, Consequences, and Cleanups.* Lanham, MD: Lexington, 2007.

Martin Meredith · *The Fate of Africa: A History of 50 Years of Independence.* New York: PublicAffairs, 2005.

Edward Miguel · *Africa's Turn?* Cambridge, MA: MIT Press, 2009.

Dambisa Moyo · *Dead Aid: Why Aid Is Not Working and How There Is a Better Way for Africa.* New York: Farrar, Straus & Giroux, 2009.

Muna Ndulo · *Democratic Reform in Africa: The Impact on Governance and Poverty Alleviation.* Athens: Ohio University Press, 2006.

Stephanie Nolen · *28 Stories of AIDS in Africa.* New York: Walker, 2007.

Paul Nugent — *Africa Since Independence: A Comparative History.* New York: Palgrave Macmillan, 2004.

Obiora Chinedu Okafor — *The African Human Rights System, Activist Forces and International Institutions.* New York: Cambridge University Press, 2007.

Abdulahi A. Osman — *Governance and Internal Wars in Sub-Saharan Africa: Exploring the Relationship.* London: Adonis & Abbey, 2007.

Steven Radelet — *Emerging Africa: How 17 Countries Are Leading the Way.* Washington, DC: Center for Global Development, 2010.

Maano Ramutsindela — *Transfrontier Conservation in Africa: At the Confluence of Capital, Politics, and Nature.* Cambridge, MA: CABI, 2007.

Jeffrey D. Sachs — *The End of Poverty: Economic Possibilities for Our Time.* New York: Penguin, 2005.

Anne Seidman, Robert B. Seidman, Pumzo Mbana, and Hanson Hu Li, eds. — *Africa's Challenge: Using Law for Good Governance and Development.* Trenton, NJ: Africa World Press, 2007.

Joseph E. Stiglitz and Andrew Charlton — *Fair Trade for All: How Trade Can Promote Development.* New York: Oxford University Press, 2005.

Ian Taylor   *China's New Role in Africa*. Boulder,
                    CO: Lynne Rienner, 2010.

Index

A

Abuja Treaty, 35
Africa
  Congress Party, 193
  country HIV/AIDS commissions, 146
  declining fortunes of, 29–38
  democratization reversals, 33–34
  dictatorial regimes, 28
  failures of government, 38
  free trade expansion needs, 39–52
  governance vs. foreign aid needs, 111–115
  improving fortunes of, 21–28
  progress without Western interference, 116–119
  protectionist policies, 48–49
  trade needs, 101–110
  US support for good governance, 113
  See also individual countries
African Endeavor project, 211
African Growth and Opportunities Act (AGOA), 59–60
African Journal of AIDS Research (2009), 130
African Peer Review Mechanism (APRM), 30, 34–35
"African Renaissance" article *(New York Times)*, 33
African Union (AU)
  African Standby Force, 211
  bi-annual meetings, 35
  creation of, 34
  deployment of peacekeepers, 210–211
  postponement of regionalism, 34–35
  regional organizations, partnerships, 206
African Union Commission, 34
AFRICOM. See US Africa Command
Afrobarometer public opinion survey project, 34
Agricultural Policy (EU), 48
AIDS
  Bush's relief program, 85
  children's expanding treatments, 166–177
  contributing social, economic factors, 139–149
  devastating effect in children, 159–165
  herbs and banana cure, 152–1554
  mother-to-infant transmission, 160–161
  overstatement of threat, 135–138
  political ignorance contributions, 150–158
  seriousness of threat, 124–134
  South African denial data, 155
  television awareness campaigns, 25
  UNAIDS report (2010), 122
  See also HIV/AIDS
Akunyili, Dora, 64–65
al-Qaeda terrorist group, 201
American Enterprise Institute, 44